What Should I Do Now?

How everyday knowledge, understanding, and wisdom answer the question.

Frederick J. Moody

Copyright © 2024 Frederick J. Moody
All rights reserved.
ISBN: 9798340154200

**DEDICATED TO:
MY FOUR SONS**

    Dave   Retired Police Sergeant. San Jose, CA
    John   Research Physicist, Livermore, CA
    Paul   Audio Forensics Expert, Sonora, CA
    Dan   Homicide Investigator, Riverside CO, CA

It was fun for me to grow up together with them. It has been even more fun as I have watched and cheered for them from the sidelines as they grew up with their own families.

ACKNOWLEDGMENT

My deep appreciation goes to Terri H. Moody for contributing her grammar and editing skills to help make this book more readable and less likely to appear written by an "illiterate engineer." (Blame uncorrected "typos" on the author.) FJM

ABREVIATED READER REACTIONS
(Complete reactions are printed at the end.)

"His writings bring up our own old memories and actions and help us laugh at ourselves for some of our actions."--*Steven A. Hucik, V. P. and Gen. Mgr. (retired), GE Hitachi Nuclear Energy.*

"Fred recounts his life lessons... wisely applying to life experiences and relationships." --*Rev. Lamar Allen, MST & M. Div.*

"You will find the right story for your current season of life."--*Dawn Standart, HR Director for large social service non-profit; wife, mother, Christian, life-long learner.*

"Whether you're seeking guidance or just a good laugh, 'What Should I Do Now?' is a must read". –*Pete O'Bryan, U. S. A.F.; Foster Farms; Nat. Cn, W & M; Distinguished Toastmaster.*

"I found the book interesting and well-written. I know the author even better now and I wish him well."--*Dick Lahey, Emeritus Prof.(RPI); Trustee, Unitarian Universalist Fellowship.*

"It was one of these books that captures your interest with a "SO WHAT" in affecting me." --*Bruce Burman, Retired VP of Semiconductor Corp.*

"I started reading it and could not put it down until I finished it!" --*Dale Isaac, Director, Audit Division California Franchise Tax Board, Retired .*

"Whenever we face some challenge in life, this is the first question we must answer." --*Dr. Shyam Dua, GENE Engineering Quality, (Ret.); Director, BWR Engineering, Westinghouse (Ret.)*

"The examples and solutions described are very practical and not just theoretical." --*Dr. David F. Kyser, Ph.D. Electrical Engineering, San Jose, CA.*

"He writes with some humor and a touch of sarcasm, and that makes him real." --*Dr. Robert A. Johns, O.D., F.A.A.O.*

"...the book offers not only entertainment but also valuable insights for navigating life's challenges."–*Sam Paulissian, Distinguished Toastmaster.*

"He brings us heart-warming snapshots of difficult circumstances..."--*David S. Licata, BS, MA, MDIV*

"...he shares timeless Biblical wisdom that will help anyone encountering similar situations..."—*Burford Furman, PhD*

"Each of the stories has a life lesson we can all relate to."-- *Sylvia Kisling, Distinguished Toastmaster, (DTM)*

"'What Should I Do Now?' is not only fun to read but also is enlightening!"—*Richard R. Schultz, Consultant, (INEL, Ret.)*

"This book should be mandatory for U. S. College English Critical Thinking Courses." –*Chris D.Hempleman, Valley Home Joint School District Board of Trustees.*

TABLE OF CONTENTS

FOREWORD ix
INTRODUCTION x

EARLY YEARS

CHAPTER 1	THE OTHER SIDE OF TOWN AND BACK......................	2
CHAPTER 2	SALESMAN MISERABLES..	7
CHAPTER 3	THE LAWNMOWER AND LADIES	11
CHAPTER 4	NECESSARY FRIEND	14
CHAPTER 5	NO TICKEE, NO WASHEE...	18
CHAPTER 6	UNBREAKABLE?	22
CHAPTER 7	MOM'S GENTLEMEN	26
CHAPTER 8	THE GUN LAP	30
CHAPTER 9	PHOTOGRAPHER *PAR EXCELLENCE*	34
CHAPTER 10	FAMILY FUN NIGHT	38

IMPRESSIONABLE YEARS

CHAPTER 11	HERO TO ZERO	44
CHAPTER 12	CHOICES?..	48
CHAPTER 13	DIRTY MACHINE SHOP	53
CHAPTER 14	FEET AND FLUOROSCOPE	56
CHAPTER 15	CONSTRUCTION WORKER	60
CHAPTER 16	MAIL CARRIER	63
CHAPTER 17	FIRST YEAR AT COLLEGE—BRAVE NEW WORLD........	67
CHAPTER 18	MAIL CARRIER, *DIFFERENT SHERIFF*.........................	73
CHAPTER 19	COLLEGE TO UNIVERSITY—A BIG STRETCH!	77
CHAPTER 20	PINSETTER—LOWEST OF THE LOW	81
CHAPTER 21	THE WINDY CITY	85

FACING THE CHALLENGES

CHAPTER 22	WEDDING BELLS	92
CHAPTER 23	LOOK BEFORE YOU LEAP	98
CHAPTER 24	SHIPWRECKED SECURITY	101
CHAPTER 25	DRAFTSMAN TO ENGINEERING ASSISTANT (?)	106
CHAPTER 26	CALIFORNIA HERE WE COME	111
CHAPTER 27	HOW DO YOU FIX THAT?	121
CHAPTER 28	WHO AM I ?	126
CHAPTER 29	THE NOT-SO-FAIR WORLD'S FAIR	131
CHAPTER 30	INDIA	135
CHAPTER 31	AN IMPORTANT VISITOR	142
CHAPTER 32	PROFESSOR: ROLE MODELS	145
CHAPTER 33	ADJUNCT—ENEMY TO ALLY	150
CHAPTER 34	LEARNING FROM STUDENTS	155
CHAPTER 35	GALLBLADDER	162
CHAPTER 36	UNREALIZED GIFT	165
CHAPTER 37	DREAM ROBBERS	168
CHAPTER 38	SELF-ROBBERY	176
CHAPTER 39	TELLING IT	185
CHAPTER 40	THE "PERFECT CRIME?"	193
CHAPTER 41	PERSPECTIVE	196

APPENDIX 204
    Seven Laws of Success 204
EPILOGUE 207
FULL READER REACTIONS 209

FOREWORD

It is a privilege to provide a foreword for Fred Moody's latest writing vignettes The second sentence of my Master's thesis was, "Recent research indicates that friendship is just as significant as therapy." On this thesis my psychologist readers wrote in bold letters, "You are right!" Fred may not be with you but he is your friend. What he has written is meant to offer his closeness to you as expressions to enhance your journey.

You may know him from his professional experience but these are what he has learned from his life travels. As you read each piece you will be amazed at how often his life experiences are meant only for your affirmation, acceptance, and inspiration. So what? That is any reader's question, isn't it? As you read Fred's experiences, pay attention to his applications. Write down your responses to the summaries of each piece. Then your experience of the friendship therapy you may need begins. Fred's authenticity is refreshing because his real-life words are for us to be encouraging on our life's adventure.—*Dr. Jeff Chapman*

INTRODUCTION

"What Should I Do Now?" is not something you ask if you're leaping to get out of the way of a speeding train! If the train is far away, you might ask, "What Should I Do Now?" assuming you can either jump into the lake on one side of the tracks, tumble down a rocky hill on the other side, or stand still on the tracks. You want to choose the action that will have the best outcome. Do you want to get soaking wet, or moan at the bottom of the hill with possible broken bones, or be smashed like a fly on the engine? If you can swim, the choice is easy.

The speeding train is an imaginary predicament. I have many true experiences where I had to ask, "What Should I Do Now?" because…

- I had a boss who did not like me;
- a respected businessman wrongly humiliated me publicly;
- my dad left our family causing me to think I was defective;
- a serious girlfriend dumped me;
- I lost two friends I could not warn of their fatal self-images;
- I was treated like the enemy after I joined a teaching staff;
- high hopes for recognition were crushed;

and there were other stressful and stretching experiences that made me ask, "What Should I Do Now?". In some cases, a speeding train would have been easier. I can swim.

The chapters in this book are approximately chronological, from my early years to the recent past. Sometimes events overlap and occasionally references are made to an event that is mentioned in a future chapter. The chapters fall naturally into three groups:

Early Years
Impressionable Years
Facing the Challenges

The episodes are self-contained so that they can be read without familiarity with other chapters; i.e., the book does not have to be read like a novel. A reader can open the book to a random chapter and read it without having read any of the others.

The episodes in this book do not revive the "POSITIVE THINKING" programs that have been popular. Nor do they revisit the "THINKING POSITIVELY" therapies that have helped many. The stories in each chapter highlight knowledge, understanding, and wisdom for ORDINARY THINKING THROUGH IDEAS and life principles to apply to our own lives.

My deep desire for this book is that it will encourage, entertain, and motivate readers of most ages, backgrounds, and frames of mind who need to know that others have gone through trials like they have faced or that they might be facing now. It is comforting to know that someone else understands what they feel—good or bad. They need to know they are not alone in their experience. Hopefully this book will bring perspective, joy, and help to find the strength needed to grow stronger, more secure, confident, and wiser in each experience.

Do not sorrow, for the joy of the Lord is your strength.
(Nehemiah 8:10b)

(All scripture references are from the New King James version of the Bible unless otherwise noted.)

EARLY YEARS

CHAPTER 1

THE OTHER SIDE OF TOWN AND BACK

An earliest memory of my dad is when I watched him use his cigarette to light something on the ground. Then he pulled me back and there was a loud "bang!" as a tin can flew way up in the air. That was my first exposure to firecrackers. We sat on the back steps and I handed him the firecrackers, which he lit and tossed into the grass while I held my ears. I remember feeling proud and important at the time, wishing it would last forever. We were close.

My dad pumped gas, checked oil, and wiped windows at my uncle's gas station while Mom kept the books. We lived with Mom's mother (my grandma) and Grandpa, Mr. Sperry.

My dad was my hero then. I'm glad my uncle waited until many years later to tell me things about my dad, like an embarrassing time brought on by his drinking problem. My dad had stopped in a bar on the way home, got drunk, and went to the men's room. He walked up behind another drunk who was finishing up at the urinal and ordered him to hand over his wallet because he had a gun. My dad took out the bills, and both men began to visit like old friends. My dad offered to buy both of them drinks with the victim's money. When they were at the bar, the victim sobered up and wanted his money back. He and my dad got into a loud argument, and the police came to settle the matter. They escorted my dad to jail. When they took off the cuffs, he turned and said to the cops, "Now I'll show you S. O. B.s how tough I really am!" My uncle bailed him out later and said he never saw anyone's face that looked so much like hamburger. (Not much bragging material there!) Even if I had known about that and my dad's other dark episodes, I still felt proud that we were pals.

Grandpa died and we moved with Grandma to a smaller house on the west side of town. I attended elementary school from kindergarten to third grade. Mom signed me up for piano lessons after school, which I hated worse than castor oil—especially when the teacher grabbed my hands and angrily banged them on the piano where they were supposed to be (mean old witch!). That was it! A week later, before my lesson started, I found a dead bird. I opened the classroom door and pitched the feathered corpse into the middle of the assembled class, jumped onto my bike, and sped away. That ended my lessons—forever, thank goodness.

As I was starting the third grade, my mom and dad added my sister Joyce to our family. Mom had explained the large bulge in her stomach, but I had a rocking horse, Lincoln Logs, an electric train, and other things that were more interesting than the prospect of a baby sister. When Joyce made her debut, they let me hold her, but I was glad it didn't become a habit. Besides, whenever I had to hold her, she either wet or pooped her diaper, or puked on me!

My mom, dad, baby sister and I moved to rent a house on the east side, which I guess was our way of becoming "independent." I went to a new school. The boys liked me because I was good at sports. It was fun hanging out with them because they had things I could put on my Christmas list. One of them had a new baseball mitt that he passed around for us to feel and try on. Another had a new bat and softball. One kid had a new headlamp for his bike and another brought a dead mouse in a jar for science class (which would not be on my list).

I learned a lot from them, like how to make a slingshot using a "Y" branch, rubber strips from an inner tube, and leather from the tongue of an old shoe. Two boys showed me how to build balsa wood model airplanes that flew with rubber band-powered propellers. Girls were still in the same category as flies and mosquitoes; useless pests in our young world.

I did have a couple of "girl" experiences in third grade. Sylvia was quiet. She sat in the row next to me. However, I kept my distance from her since she threw up all over her desk and almost doused me with no warning. I jumped out of the way in time, but it was a close call!

Another girl, Sabra, sat in front of me with pigtails that flopped onto my desk. Once I was trying to tie them in a knot without her knowing, but she whispered, "You can keep fidgeting with them!" We became friends. She liked the same things boys liked—sports, model planes, guns, stone fights. Sabra invited me to her house on Saturdays, but we had to stay outside because her mom was a night-nurse who slept all day. Once we built a fort from tree branches in a vacant lot and played "war," using our imaginations as we fought the enemy. We remained friends and talked on the phone after I moved back to the west side. Sabra and I met downtown a few times to see a movie until we reached high school.

My dad took me on his milk delivery route a few times during the summer. It was fun, especially the time he delivered milk to a small concession stand next to Phillip's Park. I waited outside while he went in for a beer. The owners had a pet monkey like one of those you see with an organ grinder, running loose and climbing trees outside. When I tried to shake hands with him, the little bastard bit my leg and ran off to the nearest tree. I picked up a heavy stick and would have bashed his head in, but it was time to go on to the next milk delivery. I got to deliver a few bottles of milk rather than kill a monkey (that deserved the death penalty)!

I got some serious news one evening. My dad drove me to the store and told me he was joining the Army Engineers to build bridges in Alaska so he wouldn't be drafted. He didn't want to fight and maybe be killed in World War II. I remember saying a tearful goodbye the afternoon he left because he wouldn't be there when I came home from school. I didn't realize that would be the last "goodbye," but not because he was "killed in action." That kind of news might have been easier on our family.

During the next months, a friend of the family—a skinny liquor-loving woman--divorced her own husband, followed my dad up to Alaska, and convinced him to divorce Mom so he could marry her (and live happily ever after, I suppose). He surrendered. Mom said she never would have agreed, so he had to get the divorce without Mom's consent. My dad and his captor got a lawyer to fix things, so Mom signed a document that was misrepresented to her. According to her, the lawyer duped her. She foolishly signed an agreement without fully understanding it. Finally, the way she described it to me was simply, "Dad isn't coming back." I thought to myself, "Sure, he's coming back! After all, I'm here!"

Many nights I could hear Mom sobbing in her bedroom. I began to think my dad divorced all of us because something's wrong with me. That took four years of counselling with Family Service to convince me otherwise. Also, several marvelous men God sent helped me overcome that self-image. My sister had the same problem, thinking, "It was a happy family until I was born. That's when they divorced." I vowed to myself that if I ever got married, I'd kill myself before ever hurting my family by a divorce. I would never abandon them no matter what. It would be easier for them if I died instead.

We had to move back to Grandma's house on the west side because my dad stopped sending money. I suspect that his new wife probably spent our rent money on liquor. Our move back to the west side was easy for me and a good thing for all of us. Grandma was happy to have human beings with her in her house—having just a pet canary was not quite enough to keep her company. We had lived at Grandma's before, and I was familiar with my previous school and surroundings. My classmates were glad to see me join them again, now in the fourth grade.

Since Mom was not receiving income or child support from my dad, she got a job in my uncle's automobile agency as office manager. (He had risen high in the business world by now with his own dealership.) While the other boys could brag about their dads, I could brag about my uncle! He was a street-smart businessman, who lived by his own rules. He showed me his brass knuckles, blackjack, and revolver which he carried in a shoulder holster—just in case a dissatisfied customer came after him! Many of the used cars he sold without any kind of warranty just made it off his lot, and that was where his responsibility ended. He was my hero through high school. But he had to move his business to Texas (because he had too many enemies in Aurora), so Mom worked for other automobile agencies. With several such jobs, she supported us and Grandma until I left for college.

During my elementary and high school years, Mom designated me "man of the house." I did all the things a man would do, like shoveling coal for the furnace, taking out ashes, shoveling snow off the sidewalks in the winter, raking and burning leaves in the fall, emptying mouse traps (sometimes cremating them in the furnace for the pure entertainment of listening to their corpses fry, bubble and crumble), cutting the grass, and making minor repairs when something broke. She paid me for these tasks so I had spending money. She also set up a Christmas savings to buy us presents every year, and she had a growing college fund for me and my sister, even though she had never gone to college.

There was a lot of growing up on the west side. Much of it came when I faced situations where I had to ask, "What Should I Do Now?"

Listen to counsel and receive instruction, that you may be wise in your latter days. There are many plans in a man's heart, nevertheless the Lord's counsel—that will stand.
(Proverbs 19: 20, 21)

> It's likely that you have lived through experiences similar to mine and have responded in a different way. But you survived. You may have scars, or you may feel that you are fortunate enough to have overcome damaging effects to your life. I think others need to know your story if you have kept it locked up. Let me urge you to share it with others. You probably cannot know in advance what a therapeutic effect it could have on someone who may be asking, "What Should I Do Now?"

CHAPTER 2

SALESMAN MISERABLES

My fourth-grade teacher said, "Tomorrow I have a big surprise for you!" That grabbed our attention. "I can't tell you what it is now, but it is something where you will be able to win some great prizes!" My mind was working at double-speed imagining some kind of contest where we could prove how fast we could run, or how many push-ups we could do or some other skill to score points and win a prize. I was good at sports, and I liked to compete, so this had to be a good thing!

The next day, most of the boys were sweaty after playing softball at lunchtime in the warm spring humidity. Girls had jumped rope and I think they had sweat, too, but they were dried out after spending a long time in their restroom. Now it was time for the teacher's surprise.

She had attended a faculty meeting where they had poisoned her mind. Now it was her job to poison our minds with the same lethal blabber. Her surprise was nothing like I was expecting or hoping for. It was an enthusiastic sales pitch!

She said we could win prizes by ringing the doorbells in our friendly neighborhoods! (She obviously didn't live in my neighborhood.) When someone answered the door, we would ask them to buy a magazine subscription to help raise money for our school. I gasped! We had to ring doorbells? We had to sell magazine subscriptions? I hated the idea! Every kid was expected to do it out of *loyalty* to the school! I had no choice. "What should I do now?" I wanted to pick up my books and transfer to another school. But she said that all the other schools were doing it too—(conducting the same "death march!"). A transfer would be futile.

The only way out of this was to die! Maybe running away would be a better idea, but I would miss my dog. I could pretend to be sick and stay home, but I would miss lunch hour softball. There had to be another way to get out of this doorbell selling.

Ringing doorbells with a friend was fun at night when it was dark. We rang a doorbell and ran to hide where we could watch the porch light go on, the door open, and someone step out looking for the ringer! And I did not have to sell a magazine subscription!

I examined the list of prizes. There was nothing that would drive me to ring a single doorbell! A softball mitt (I had one), a pogo stick, a tea set, an overnight bag with wheels. Yuck! The prizes were bait. The other kids took the bait and were crazy with excitement about winning a prize. They could hardly wait for school to be over so they could start ringing doorbells. They were like dumb, wild animals lured into a cage! Not me!

The teacher handed out clipboards and sales forms. I wanted to burn mine. But she would want them back. Pretending to lose them might work, but I did not want to lie and make God mad at me. I needed a different escape route. What Should I Do Now?

The teacher demonstrated with one of the girls, showing how easy it would be to sell a magazine subscription.
The girl pretended to knock at an invisible door and the teacher pretended to open it.

"Yes, little girl. What do you want?"
The girl said, "I'm from Mary A. Todd School and we are having a magazine sale to help raise money for our school. Would you like to buy a magazine subscription to help us?"
The teacher answered, "Let me see what magazines are for sale."
The girl handed her a list.
"I think I would like a subscription to this magazine."
They pretended to do the paperwork.

Then the teacher turned to the class and said, "See how simple it is?"

I thought, "Why don't you take my clipboard and other junk and ring doorbells for me? You'd make two of us happy—you and me!" But I kept my mouth shut.

After school we were turned loose on unsuspecting neighborhood victims to start the doorbell raid. I had devised my own sales pitch which I believed would spare me agony, and cut conversations short with whoever answered the door. My shaking finger rang the first doorbell. An older gentleman opened it.

"Hi, kid. What d'ya want?"
I said, "You don't want to buy a magazine, do you?"
He said, "Oh, h*** no! I've got more magazines than I can read now."
Then he shut the door. I thought, "It worked! That's good! I hope they all go like that!"

I used the same speech on the others.
"You don't want to buy a magazine, do you?"
One slammed the door and shouted, "No!" at the same time.
I thought, "That's fine with me."

At the start of each school day, every kid reported how many contacts he or she had made and how many subscriptions they had sold. "12 contacts with seven subscriptions!" "Eight contacts with five subscriptions." When it came to me, "Lots of contacts and they all said 'No.'" Same report every day until the agony was over. No subscriptions—no prizes—but surprisingly an "honorable mention" and a feeling that I beat the system.

Now after many years, I see the doorbell ringing-magazine selling episode as a good thing—a stretching thing! If I didn't step out of familiar surroundings because I thought I wouldn't like it, or I was simply afraid of the unexpected, how would I ever allow new experiences into my life? I think most of us grow by new experiences. The doorbell-magazine-experience must have planted seeds to make me stronger for when I would have to face uncertainties. I didn't win prizes selling magazines, but in another sense, I actually did win.

***I sought the Lord and He heard me, and delivered me from all my fears** (Psalm 34:4)*

> There must have been times where you were forced to do something—a task, a duty, a commitment that you passionately did not want to do, but there was no easy (or hard) way to get out of it. How did you handle that? And what was your view of the matter after you finished it? Others need to know so they can identify with you.

CHAPTER 3

THE LAWNMOWER AND LADIES

I was "man of the house," living with three women—Mom, Grandma, and my little sister. Mom worked at an automobile office to support our family. I did the heavy lifting which included cutting the grass. Mom paid me thirty-five cents for that, which was above minimum wage. We had two push-mowers in the garage without grass-catchers, so the cut grass flew back and hit my knees. Sometimes I didn't see a hazard in time and churned up a smelly pile that a sick dog dumped, which stuck to my overalls and shoes. I hurried to the garden hose to clean off my shoes, pants and the mower blades after each canine encounter. A neighbor showed me how to oil a lawnmower and sharpen the blades. I learned a lot about machines from those mowers and became an expert grass-cutter!

    Not everyone will appreciate it, but grass-cutting is an art, especially with a push-mower. It's a skill you develop with practice. You cut a straight row from one end of a yard to the other, and then you use that row as a guide to cut a row next to it in the other direction. Back and forth, each time using the last row to guide the next row. Small errors in each row add up, and the final row might be as crooked as a dog's hind leg compared to the first row! But all my mistakes were covered by the blanket of grass that flew out behind the mower. Besides, each blade of grass was cut short and that was the reason for mowing in the first place. Mission accomplished!

    Three widows in the neighborhood asked if I would cut their lawns—for money. I agreed if they would keep their dogs in the house. They said I could use their garden hoses to clean off my mower, pants and shoes if necessary. Some neighbors owned cats, which didn't leave any mess in the grass. I realized that cats had private collection boxes but I didn't know what the owners did with the contents, and I didn't want to know.

Information travels fast, and more widows hired me to cut their grass. Some even wanted it raked after cutting—for extra cash. Every week during summer I was rollin' in dough, and I had a considerable territory of widow clients within a few blocks. They called me! I didn't have to ring doorbells to sell magazines, either! But there was a problem. Several widows had inherited large lawns and they were poor, without money to hire a gardener. They paid me in pennies and nickels, far less than Mom paid me for our small lawn. "Thank you," they said with a big smile as I was dripping with sweat. I would think, "I worked my butt off for this?" as I pocketed the few coins.

I didn't want to go back to those places. But they kept calling every week during the summer for me to please come and cut their grass again. I am sure I wondered, "What Should I Do Now?" I wanted a good reason not to go. Maybe I could find another kid to do it, but I was the only one in the neighborhood. Who else could do it? My conscience wouldn't let me ignore the grey-haired ladies, so my lawnmower and I begrudgingly rolled over to their homes. Again I would get a "Thank you," and a warm smile, and a few coins. But it was beginning to bother me less and less.

This is the best part: A strange, warm feeling developed in my chest that I had never felt before when I stood on the doorstep of one grey-haired lady to collect. She reached into her little black purse and paid me with the few pennies and nickels she had saved. A smile came over her wrinkled face and she whispered, "Thank you."

I was not the same after that. And so it was with the other widows—a few carefully saved coins, a sweet smile showing heartfelt gratitude, and a soft, "Thank you."

I realized that I would be willing to cut their grass for no pay at all, just to have them smile and say "Thank you!" There was no price tag for the genuine gratitude coming from their hearts and going to mine. God must have been shaping my sensitivity to others who needed my help. Helping older people was infinitely more rewarding than hearing someone who answered my knock at his door say, "No, I don't want any magazine subscriptions."

Then the king will say, "I'm telling the solemn truth: Whenever you did one of these things (cared for the hungry, thirsty, sick, needy, etc.) to someone overlooked or ignored, that was me—you did it to me." *(St. Matthew 25:45b, The Message)*

> Can you recall a time when you felt unhappy about having to face an unwanted assignment, and something happened to completely reverse your feelings? Explain what happened.

CHAPTER 4

NECESSARY FRIEND

My best friend Terry was acting silly after lunch before fifth grade art class. The teacher had not arrived and most of the kids were gathered around him, laughing as he stood on a chair wrapping the cord of a window shade around his neck like he was going to hang himself. Terry was the most popular boy in class—smart, athletic, and friendly. He and I were "best friends" and I joined the frivolity, pretending to nudge the chair he was standing on—but horror of horrors! It made him lose balance, almost tearing down the cord and shade. The fearful look on his face suddenly was real! He unwound the cord and got off the chair. All the kids laughed, but not Terry. He glared at me!

The teacher came into the room and everyone hurried to their desks. Terry kept glaring at me. I said, "I'm sorry. I didn't mean to…" but he looked away. I can feel again the tightening fear, panic, and pain that gripped me every minute. Terry was my best friend and I had done a terrible thing to him. It was like I had accidentally killed my best friend and I didn't know how to bring him back to life! My mind had to be whirling with, "What Shall I Do Now?"

As soon as the bell rang ending the class, I rushed over to Terry and begged him to forgive me, but he put his things away and ignored me without a word. I couldn't stand his silence. Now, many years later, I can understand my state of mind at the time. I needed Terry. Every kid in the class was his friend, but I especially needed him for *my* friend. Having him for a friend gave me a feeling of importance I desperately needed. Counselors later told me that being accepted by someone who was popular gave me security, which had been partly destroyed by a father who did not see enough value in me to stick around. The one person who should have been the most important man in the world to me had rejected me! I needed acceptance. Terry had accepted me—until now. I begged him to forgive me. In desperation, I thought I could buy him back. "Would a few dollars make things OK?" I asked. That was all the money I had in my possession. (By today's scale, it would have amounted to several hundred dollars.) He turned and walked out of the room. I felt like crying! (No one had ever mentioned that you cannot buy true friendship.)

I never felt worse pain than on that day. It was not physical like when you fall off your bike onto the cement, or get hit in the face with a softball. It was pain you can feel many years later almost as if it just happened! Crushing pain! Even when my wife died, the pain was softer. The pain in fifth grade was one of *rejection* by a best friend. Emotional pain they say hurts in your head, but still makes you hurt everywhere else at the same time. I can understand why people can reach a point where life is not worth living and take the final escape. Wanting to die when my best friend rejected me was a sure way to stop the pain, but I was not smart enough to know how to kill myself at that age. I did not want to keep on living if Terry did not accept me as a friend. It did not matter that other kids liked me. It did not matter that I was a good student—or the fastest runner, or that I had interesting and exciting hobbies—or that I had my heart set on a bright future. The only thing that mattered was that my best friend rejected me and life was empty.

There was one person who would listen and maybe help—Mr. Warner, our principal, a man God sent into my life to be a substitute dad on several occasions. I went to his office. He could always see students immediately. When he asked if anything was wrong, I answered, half-sobbing, "Terry doesn't like me." Mr. Warner took it from there. He was familiar with these things and said, "Leave it to me." Later that afternoon, Terry was called out of class to the principal's office. When the last class was over that day, Terry came to me and said that he really was my friend and he knew I didn't intend any harm to him. That was that. My pain disappeared.

It continued to bother me that I had gone into an emotional tailspin because of a friendship with one person. Another thing bothered me. What if I said or did something else that would make Terry mad and he would reject me again? Was this a friendship where I had to walk on eggshells? Also, what if he ever moved away, or died? I could lose him some other way besides rejection. Moving away or death was not the same as rejection. Rejection was a constant fear. I determined that I never wanted to hurt anyone by rejecting them!

About that time a new boy joined our class—Ken. He had a friendly smile, was red headed, and polite, but none of the kids included him at recess or other activities. Ken stood by himself while others were busy with each other, playing games or assembling in closed groups. Ken was rejected—probably not on purpose, but no one was friendly enough to speak to him.

If I needed Terry as a friend, maybe someone needed me as a friend. Maybe Ken needed a friend. I walked home from school with him one day (it was only a block out of the way). Before we went far, we were talking about similar interests. Ken liked to write stories, and so did I. We later collaborated on a play, which we showed to our teacher. She liked it and wanted us to choose class members to be in it. She let us perform it for the class. Ken ceased to become a wallflower after that. Later he became our class president!

Terry and I remained friends, but when I discovered the importance of his friendship to me, I realized that someone else out there also needed me as a friend. I no longer had to walk on eggshells to protect a friendship. Real friends can overlook our missteps, and they are quick to forgive when necessary.

My fifth-grade experience showed me that the most intense pain I ever experienced was *rejection*—being forsaken by a best friend, even for a short time. The cause of the pain was my dependence on a friend for security, status, self-worth, and value, and then losing it all by rejection. But the outcome of that agonizing experience was that I realized *someone else needed me as a friend.* That's when I took a step to be a friend to another person so they would not have to feel *rejected*.

The Bible tells of One who suffered the ultimate rejection:

He was in the world, and the world was made through Him, and the world did not know Him. He came to His own, and His own did not receive Him. (*John 1:10, 11*)

He is despised and rejected by men, a Man of sorrows and acquainted with grief…
But He was wounded for our transgressions, He was bruised for our iniquities, The chastisement for our peace was upon Him, and by His stripes we are healed. (*Isaiah 53: 3, 5*)

But not everyone rejected Him:

But as many as received Him, to them He gave the right to become children of God, to those who believe in His name: who were born, not of blood, nor of the will of the flesh, nor of the will of men, but of God. **(John 1:12, 13)**

A man who has friends must himself be friendly, but there is a friend who sticks closer than a brother. (*Proverbs 18:24*)

> Did you ever have a close friend that profoundly disappointed you? How did you handle it? Did you lose or keep your friendship? What did you learn? Others need to know.

CHAPTER 5

NO TICKEE, NO WASHEE

The auditorium lights dimmed and a dozen of us middle school boys waited nervously backstage for the signal. We were Mr. Whiting's tumbling class from the YMCA, invited to perform a gymnastics skit to entertain a group of Aurora's business leaders. The stage lights came up. "OK, boys, you're on!"

That was my signal to skip onto the stage whistling, dressed in a white tunic and nylon skull-cap with a three-foot braided pigtail made from stockings my mother had donated to this *keep-her-kid-off-the-street* activity. I carried a bushel basket overflowing with laundry and dumped it on a cafeteria table center stage between two high-jump poles with a rope clothesline strung between them. I began to hang clothes on the line as a customer walked on stage with a large tee-shirt. He sniffed it and held his nose. I gave him a ticket, took the shirt, and he walked out.

After hanging up more clothes, I changed a sign that said "TODAY" to another which said "TOMORROW." The same customer returned and motioned for his shirt. I motioned that I needed his ticket. He motioned that he did not have it. I spoke the only audible lines in the whole skit: "No Tickee, No Washee!" The customer pounded the table with his fists. He shook both fists at me. I made a quick search for his shirt and found it. He held it up and it had shrunk to baby size.

The customer began to chase me around the table. Other customers entered, and tried to protect me, but he chased them, too. From then the skit became a wild chase around the stage. All of us performed tricks on a long matt which was rolled across the front of the stage while we were being chased. Forward rolls, backward rolls, cartwheels, handsprings, and leapfrog rolls. The audience, mostly moms and businessmen, cheered and clapped.

For a finale, one boy got down on his hands and knees at the near end of the mat while the rest of us ran and dived over him, each one hitting the matt in a somersault. A second boy got on his hands and knees next to the first boy, so next we had to dive over two boys. Then a third boy. Finally, six boys were lined up together. For a last jumping dive, five more boys were added and I was supposed to dive over eleven boys, a seeming impossible feat! I ran as fast as I could to the row of eleven bodies and, at the last instant, they all rose up on their hands and feet, making an arched tunnel so I could scoot under them and come out the other end! We all took a bow, and the curtain closed to a standing ovation.

When I had started Mr. Whiting's tumbling class two years before, I did not know how to perform some of the tricks he taught us. I thought, "I don't think I will ever be able to do that!" But he took me and the other boys and patiently worked hours with us every Wednesday after school to teach us how. He spotted us so we didn't hurt ourselves, and he encouraged us by telling us what good progress we were making.

There were advanced tumblers who did tricks that were way beyond anything I could achieve. If you watch Olympic competition, those tumblers were doing some of the same tricks those competitors do, both on the ground, on parallel bars, and hanging rings. Some could run up to the matt, start with a handspring, twisting in mid-air to land facing backwards (it's called a "round-off") but their high momentum kept them going with a series of back handsprings the length of the matt, one after another, until they reached the end, where they leaped high into the air for a back summersault before coming down for a perfect two-point landing on their feet. When I mentioned to Mr. Whiting I could never do that, he said, "I'll show you how. In three or four months you'll be able to do that—and more." I thought, "He must think he can teach me how to fly! When he finds out I am a hopeless case—'What Should I do Now?' I hate to be the first person he will ever have to point to and say I made him give up!"

But I remember how he taught me to do a back handspring. He got down on his knees, stood me in front of him facing to his left. Then he said, "Slowly pretend like you are sitting down in a chair, keeping your back straight and your arms hanging straight down. When you feel yourself begin to fall backwards, spring as high as you can upward, while throwing your arms, chest, and head backwards." After several hundred attempts, I began to land on my hands! My feet followed, and I was ready to do a second one—then a third! How about doing a back summersault in mid-air? It was easier than a back handspring! A front summersault in mid-air was harder than a back one! All of those tricks looked so far beyond my gymnastic ability and coordination that, left to myself, I would not even have attempted them without Mr. Whiting's insisting that he could show me how and I could do it. He made it possible for me to go beyond what I ever thought I could have done.

I believe Frank Whiting was one of the men God sent into my life to guide me through a major turning point. I could only see myself in a limited capacity. There were levels in life I did not believe I could ever achieve. My strength, ability, or other resources were not enough to qualify me for some things I wished I could do. Logically, I should have abandoned my desire for those things. But Mr. Whiting had a different view. He knew that he could help me go beyond what I thought I could do or become. With his help, guidance, knowledge, and encouragement, he helped me exceed my self-imposed limitations. I wanted to be like him. I wanted to do for others what he did for me. I want to continue helping others go beyond themselves, becoming more than they ever thought they could be, living lives of fulfillment beyond what they thought was possible.

A biblical truth explains exactly what Mr. Whiting did for me, but extends it to every walk of life to anyone who will accept it:

Now to Him who is able to do exceedingly abundantly above all that we ask or think, according to the power that works in us, to Him be glory in the church by Christ Jesus to all generations, forever and ever. Amen. (*Ephesians 3:20, 21*)

> Can you acknowledge one person or couple who, in some way, enabled you to "go beyond yourself," whether it has been your schooling, career, or personal growth? Can you be that person to someone else you think of?

CHAPTER 6

UNBREAKABLE?

The boys in middle school shop had to pick a project—some wooden object to make with saws, sanders, lathes, joiners, and all sorts of equipment. The result would be a fine creation that the boys and their families would be proud of. It was not in my DNA to build wooden objects that had fine details, like picture frames, end tables, or lampstands.

Mr. T. showed us how to use all the tools without amputating part of ourselves. Some boys chose to make small tables or cabinets. A few made picture frames. None of the usual projects interested me—too much detail. Each one required measurements, cutting, sanding, fitting, and varnishing to produce nicely crafted things that their parents would "Ooooh, and Ahhh" over while they found a prominent place in their homes to display their son's ingenuity. Even if I created a sleek piece of furniture, it would not fit in with our home décor of triple-painted dining room chairs and rustic, dilapidated furniture. Even our rugs had gaping holes (until I salvaged the old, but still almost-new carpeting from a friend when his parents had their house re-carpeted). As I watched my classmates eagerly working with tools, it gave me morbid satisfaction thinking that their fancy projects would someday become kindling when they grew up and left home. Also, everything they made was breakable, but I had an idea for something *un*breakable!

An article in *Popular Mechanics* magazine showed how to make a rope. You needed a big ball of binder's twine, four hand drills fitted with hooks, and four people to operate the drills. The teacher discouraged my proposed project, but when I told him I wanted to make something unbreakable, he became interested. He had never made a rope and he followed each step, even helping me enlist four other boys in the project.

Binder twine was used in those days to tie up packages for mailing. One strand could hold about 50 pounds. The first step was to assemble 10 strands of twine 100 feet long, making a cord tied at each end. One end of this cord was attached to a hook on one of the small drills. The method is sketched below. Two additional cords were made and attached to the hooks on the other two small drills. The opposite ends of the three cords were attached to the large hook fitted in the large drill.

A strong boy held the large drill with the large hook that now had three separate cords attached to it as shown in the sketch. Each cord extended 100 feet to separate hooks at the far end in the three drills held by three other boys, who began to turn their respective drills clockwise in rhythm together, pulling tightly on the cords. When the cords were tightly twisted, the three boys stopped twisting and the boy at the other end began to turn the large drill in the opposite direction, twisting the three cords together in a tight braid which progressed from his location to the other end where the three cords were then cut free from the small drills and tied to form the entire rope. With the three cords attempting to untwist in one direction and the entire braid of three attempting to untwist in the other direction, the rope was stable and tight.

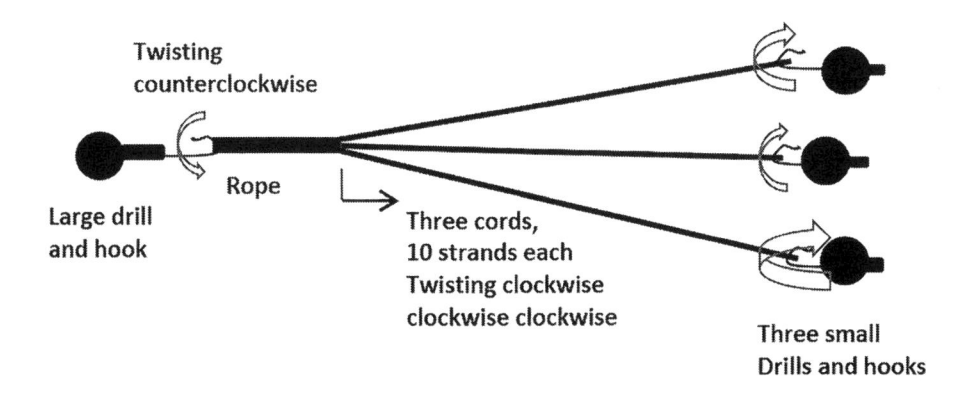

Twisting counterclockwise

Rope

Large drill and hook

Three cords, 10 strands each Twisting clockwise clockwise clockwise

Three small Drills and hooks

The whole class took turns pulling the rope in opposite directions, proving it was "unbreakable." I took my "unbreakable" rope home while the other boys had to delicately transport their projects, trying not to drop them because of their fragility! I did have one remaining problem: how to tie one end of the rope to the thick branch from a huge oak tree at the corner of our back yard. The branch was so high I was afraid to climb the tree. Until I could solve this problem, my "unbreakable" rope sat idle. A friend got a hot idea! We tied a long piece of string to a stone and after many throws, it went up and over the branch, pulling the string as it came down. I tied one end of the rope to the string, pulled it up over the branch far enough to make a slip knot, inserted the free end, and pulled it up again. After making a foot loop and cutting off the excess, the rope swing was ready for action.

Every kid in the neighborhood, and also my mom, took turns swinging from the porch way across the yard and back, a distance over 50 feet in one direction. Two or three kids could swing at one time, the rope was so strong—"unbreakable!"

Today there are different rope designs, but King Solomon referred to the three-cord rope in the 10th century B.C. when he wrote,

A threefold cord is not easily broken. (Ecclesiastes 4:12)

I have wondered what the king was telling us in those few short words. I think he was too wise just to be giving a lesson in arithmetic—how three cords are stronger than one. Too obvious. What else could he be showing us? As I have pondered the statement with other comments by King Solomon, one answer that makes sense is accountability. Two people can decide to be accountable to each other and trust each other in all circumstances, but to have a third person who knows both of them and is strong enough to hold both of them accountable makes their relationship secure.

The number "three" in Solomon's words may have spiritual significance to a bride and groom. They make wedding vows to God, Who is the third cord in their threefold "rope." They make their vows to each other and to God for accountability. Married couples I know who fit the threefold accountability have reached their 40, 50, and 60th anniversaries.

One of my friends is a retired private investigator (PI) who often was hired by husbands or wives to learn if their spouse was having a secret affair. The accountability cord was missing from their marriage. They may have claimed to be accountable to each other, but most of us have weaknesses and we need those who will hold us accountable.

When Phyllis and I knew that our friendship had reached a lifetime commitment stage where we wanted to be forever true to each other, I realized how fragile love is and how it needed to be protected. I felt that I had to write a "commitment note" on the back of her graduation picture that she carried in her purse. She could read it if she ever had doubts about us. Not knowing much scripture or even giving God credit for bringing us together at the time, my note said, "Phyllis and I are not guarding our love for each other alone. God is guarding it with us." Deep inside, I had to put our relationship into the hands of One Who I knew was bigger and stronger than either of us for accountability.

***For the ways of man are before the eyes of the Lord, and He ponders all his paths* (Proverbs 5:21)**

> Try to remember a commitment you made to (1) another person; (2) an organization; (3) to yourself; (4) or to God. Did you feel compelled to keep that commitment or was it easy to break? What caused you to keep it or break it? Were there rewards or consequences?

CHAPTER 7

MOM'S GENTLEMEN

The young woman smiled as she began her Toastmasters speech. "Good morning! I'm Eleanor, and I am six years happily divorced!" Her speech was a short personal story, including pride in her naval officer son, her job as an IT specialist, and overseas trips for her company to places where she could include vacation days and several once-in-a-lifetime excursions.

My antennas went up when she said, "happily divorced." I wondered why someone could be happy about being divorced. I knew there were women who were glad to be loosed from husbands who were abusive, narcissistic, unloving, neglectful, selfish, critical, violent, drunkards or drug users. But those were few. Most of the divorced people I knew were unhappy about it, and some were heartbroken. Most couples did not separate on mutually happy terms. One wanted the divorce and the other didn't. So it was with my own mother.

When a lawyer mailed Mom the final divorce papers, which had been obtained by deception, we had adjusted to a new life at Grandma's house. Mom had a job as office manager at an automobile agency to support all of us in exchange for living with Grandma. She was good at her job of keeping the financial records because she had taken finance and secretarial courses in high school. She never attended college; it was her mission to send both of her children to college. Mom was a voracious reader with a library of two large, overfilled book cases. She knew a lot about many things and could hold an intelligent conversation with most people, regardless of their academic standing. She carried herself with confidence and poise, but was always friendly and caring for even the smallest needs of those in her business or even in our neighborhood. No person was too small for her to hold back her full attention and service. She introduced me to Paul J., an Afro-American auto mechanic who had trained in the Olympic trials with the track star Jesse Owens. Paul coached me on how to run and win the 440-yard dash in high school. (I hasten to say, he coached me on how not to come in last).

Mom was an attractive woman, so it was no surprise that various gentlemen visited in their sleek automobiles at Grandma's house to give Mom a ride to work, and to bring her home in the evening. One gentleman was Earl, who appeared with increasing frequency as the weeks passed. He became a fixture on weekends. From my fifth-grade view, I could see that Mom was his primary interest, and that my sister and I were inconvenient baggage. I saw how other dads treated their kids. It was easy to see that Earl was a creep, although I didn't speak up. To impress my mom he took me shopping to buy a gasoline model airplane once. He left it to me to get the thing running. Adjusting it took adult guidance. When Earl appeared, I asked him to help. Impatient, short-tempered—I had sidetracked him. He came to see my mom, not to waste time with a smelly model plane engine. "We'll try to figure it out Saturday." I was thinking, "He doesn't care—He'll figure a way to get out of it!" And he did.

I know I was confused over how I should react about this man. I must have been asking myself, "What should I do now?" Should I tell Mom how I felt about Earl? That he was a bluffer who didn't care one bit for me and my sister, and that he was just putting on a show? Would that be selfish if she liked the guy? Would I be destroying her prospects for future happiness when I was grown up and left home someday? It turned out that I didn't have to do anything. Apart from all the drooling interest he showed for my mom, she must have recognized that he had no real interest in her kids, so she dumped him. Three cheers for Mom!

Within two months, Earl had moved into the house of a divorced mother whose daughter was in my class. I could have asked her if Earl had to buy her a World War 2 Kewpie Doll and give her spending money to keep her distance, but I didn't. I never offered my opinion of Earl to my mom. She knew what a crumb he really was without my report.

Les was a gentleman who devoted himself to helping others. He not only chauffeured Mom to work and back, but he went out of his way to ask Grandma if he could take her anywhere. He did not seem to have matrimony on his mind. He noticed that Grandma's house was badly in need of paint so he painted it for only the cost of paint (that was his business). Often Les took Mom, me, and my sister out on a Sunday afternoon drive to a park, ending up at a restaurant where he treated us to dinner. His mother lived in his house where he saw to her care and comfort. Once he asked if I would be willing to escort his very shy niece to a teenagers dance, which I did. Barbara was a dainty girl, but shy, as he said. I did most of the talking, asking questions. But she enjoyed our date, and I thought I made someone happy that evening. Les was always there to help our family when needed, expecting nothing in return.

One final significant gentleman was Chuck. He had a medical discharge from the war, having been wounded by a shattered wooden bullet, and he was living with constant abdominal pain. He was able to work as a mechanic while supporting his mother, and he also gave Mom rides wherever she needed to go. He could fix anything that needed repair—plumbing, electrical, gas stove, furnace, and my used 1940 Chevy which Mom managed to purchase for $150 from her agency for my high-school graduation present. Chuck and I overhauled it in Grandma's driveway. It had been owned by one elderly lady who said she only used it to drive to the grocery store and back. With 100,000 plus miles, I wondered which store! He was another kind man who was always ready to help, expecting nothing in return. When Phyllis and I married, Chuck insisted that we use his newer Nash Rambler for our wedding trip from Aurora, Illinois to Boulder, Colorado where I would enroll in the University. He drove my Chevy until we returned. That was his wedding gift to us.

Phyllis and I moved to Boulder right after the wedding where I started classes and Phyllis found a job. My sister was also off to college in Kansas for a degree in Social Work. Mom was the driving motivator that pushed us to academia. She was left with Grandma keeping the house. There was no hint of other gentlemen pursuing her, probably because Mom made it plain that she had no intention of ever marrying again. One crash and burn experience was enough. She kept phone numbers of several gentlemen of unblemished character that she could call if necessary.

Grandma got sick, went to the hospital, and died. Within two years, Mom moved to a mobile home park near us in San Jose. She enjoyed spending time with her four grandsons and attending many family events before succumbing to MS and a bleeder in her brain that they couldn't stop.

Mom survived the crushing blow of an unexpected, unwanted divorce when she had thought she had the stable, happy family she had hoped for. She had a broken heart, but still had the resilience to raise a young son and younger daughter, making sure we were exposed to good adults who were model examples in school and youth activities. She was the protective mother hen who would not risk our well-being in favor of the potential happiness and security she might have found with a second marriage. And because of her love and countless sacrifices, both my sister and I have enjoyed careers and fulfillment in life that Mom only dreamed of. Thanks, Mom.

She watches over the ways of her household, and does not eat the bread of idleness. Her children rise up and call her blessed; (Proverbs 31:27-28a)

> You may be a single parent by death, divorce, or other means, but the care of your children is your deep concern. Recognizing that each family situation is unique, if you had to list your two or three most pressing concerns as a single parent, what would they be? Can you explain how you would face them, e. g. friends, prayer, agencies, etc.?

CHAPTER 8

THE GUN LAP

Steve Prefontaine was in the lead as the runners approached the final lap of the 10,000 meter (6.2 mile) run. They came around the far curve in a 1976 International Track Meet. Suddenly a runner from West Africa sprinted past him, raising his arms in victory as he crossed the original starting line. The starter fired his gun signaling "one lap to go," or the "gun lap." That runner staggered onto the grassy midfield and collapsed. Prefontaine kept running with a puzzled expression. One more lap to complete the distance! The West African had quit the race one lap too soon! He didn't realize he was one lap short of reaching the finish line!

That scene describes some of my endeavors—projects I worked hard to complete, but they never reached the finish line! Maybe someday…

Patty was standing in front of her house with a young couple and their baby when I rode by on my bike. She called, "Fred! This is my brother I told you about!" I stopped and hurried up to the sidewalk. She proudly introduced the young man in khakis. His wife stood beside him holding their baby girl. "Bill draws pictures like you do." Patty was in fifth grade, and I was an eighth grader at the same school. She liked my weekly comic strip that I tacked on the bulletin board outside the principal's office—*The Adventures of Raggs Rabbit*. I drew each strip myself and invented a continuing story. Every strip ended with the hero in danger or something terrible about to happen. That device brought kids back to read the next week's installment.

Bill had just finished army service and now he and his family were living in an upstairs apartment over Patty's family. "So you like to draw comic strips!" Bill said to me. I affirmed. I sensed an immediate connection. He went on, "I do too! Let me see some of your work!" I hurried to my house across the street and got a dozen comic strips. Bill studied them. He said he liked my ideas and complimented me on my India ink drawings. I was flattered that he wanted to keep them a few days.

Ours was a lopsided friendship, since Bill was a married father in his twenties and I was in eighth grade! But we hit it off well. Two days later, he surprised me with a full-size, professional-looking comic strip page. It had 12 square panels (separate frames) outlined in black. It was like an uncolored Sunday edition of a *Rags Rabbit* adventure, all drawn with black India ink. I was overjoyed! I could see that this sample comic strip art was better quality than what appeared in any newspapers I ever saw—*The Chicago Tribune*—*The Chicago Sunday Times*—*The Aurora Beacon News!*

Bill admitted he was not a storyteller. He proposed that I could write the stories and he would do the illustrating. This was a new dream! Bill would be the artist and I would be the brains of the story line! My English teachers told me that I was a good storyteller, and now I could capitalize on that! I would continue the eighth-grade comic strip while learning all I could working with Bill. When a major newspaper gave us a contract for the strip, it would be with "K and M Productions," (K standing for Kelly and M standing for Moody). Ahhh! Fame!

Bill found a job to support his family and drew comic strips in the evening. By fall, we had a stack of *Raggs Rabbit* stories, ready for newspaper publication. We had to find the right newspaper—that is, any newspaper. That was Bill's job, him being the older and wiser businessman (well, older, anyway). His wife tried to help him write letters on plain white stationery to editors of major newspapers, offering them a fresh, new comic strip.

In the serious business world, you need letterhead stationery. I learned that later from my uncle, a used car dealer, who sent his secretary to buy a replacement spotlight from a lightbulb store. She asked for a dealer's discount. The store owner told her he couldn't give a discount unless my uncle was in the electrical business. She said he was. The owner demanded proof. She told my uncle, who then had special stationary printed that said,

> King Electronic Industries
> Electric Chairs a Specialty

She got the spotlight—and the discount after explaining that after so many uses, those chairs do wear out.

Neither Bill nor his wife knew a thing about the comic strip market, and they didn't have any marketing skills. The editors didn't have time for anyone with something to sell, unless it was advertising, especially double-page! There had to be another way, but getting a comic strip published seemed impossible unless you were the editor! They didn't know about agents, and they didn't know where to get help. My dream of fame and fortune was fading. If I wondered, "What should I do now?" I didn't come up with any answers.

School started and I spent less time with Bill. My *Raggs Rabbit* comic strip continued to be posted outside the principal's office, but the version targeted for public newspapers is probably stashed in someone's garage or has been recycled in a landfill. It never happened—not because it wasn't worthy of publication (my opinion) but because we didn't know how to sell it to an editor of a newspaper. We didn't realize there was a *gun lap*.

I learned a lot from Bill, but I also learned a hard lesson: we can produce a prize-winning product or process, but if we don't know how to distribute, advertise, sell, promote it, or otherwise make it available to others, we can die holding it in our possession, unreleased, unshared, and whatever good it could have done for others will die with us. We need to have a plan in place for releasing or distributing the product or process where it can accomplish its intended purpose as soon as we finish the *gun lap*.

Without counsel, plans go awry, but in the multitude of counselors they are established. (Proverbs 15:22)

>Did you ever pursue a planned program or activity with high expectations, only to discover that you had failed to complete the plan? That is, there were unintended consequences you would have discovered if you had planned the program or activity to its finish. If so, what did you do and/or what did you learn that would be helpful to the rest of us? If we are following God's plan, are we likely to experience "unintended consequences?"

CHAPTER 9

PHOTOGRAPHER *PAR EXCELLENCE*

I couldn't guess what was in the Christmas package from Mom, but I knew It would be surprising things for me to learn about. Those were the kind of gifts she picked for me and my sister with her limited budget. When the wrapping paper came off, the label on the box read, "Black-and-White Film Developing Kit."

That gift launched me on a hobby that lasted over 50 years. Imagining that I would be able to take pictures and print them myself was fun and challenging. I began the process right away. Whenever I developed pictures under a red light in my makeshift darkroom, I could feel my heart racing as I watched the images appear. No more waiting a week for the drug store to get the prints back!

Throughout high school I developed rolls of film and made contact prints in my room. Later I bought a used enlarger and set up a darkroom in a basement fruit-cellar. Mom bought a camera that used *Speed Midget* gas-filled flash bulbs. Sometimes they exploded with a loud "pop." I had to warn older people about this, since I did not have insurance to cover accidental death from scaring someone out of their wits! Soon, with my growing photography business I was making family photo Christmas cards, portraits of old and young people and children, and even one ugly, pedigreed bulldog, slobbers and all! People paid me for prints of all sizes including mounted and framed 11 by 14-inch family portraits at bargain prices!

One evening the owner/editor-in-chief (I call him "Mr. Newsman") of a local newspaper phoned because he heard that I developed film. Could I develop pictures for his newspaper? It was an emergency and he needed prints by 8:00 AM the next morning to meet a deadline. I agreed, even though it meant working into the night. Mom warned me about this man. He was on the city council, a so-called "wheeler-dealer," and one of the most disliked politicians in Aurora. He was against every good idea proposed, and used his newspaper to publish his negative views. But developing pictures was my business. I didn't have to know about the customer, although I wish I had known about the man at the time.

An overweight, balding, cigar-puffing figure parked his car in front of our house within the hour and handed me a film-pack. He said he would collect the pictures at eight AM. I had never seen a film-pack before! It was a metal box the size of a deck of cards. I shook it and heard the films inside, but I didn't know how to get them out. "What should I do now?"

I instantly thought of William, the high-school "nerd," a kid one year ahead of me. He carried the only slide rule on campus, attached to his belt, and he sometimes taught math classes when the teacher was absent. William had his own photography business, using a speed-graphic camera (like news reporters carried). His main customers were families at funerals, who wanted a picture of their departed loved one in their last repose before the lid was closed. He told me how to open the film pack so I was able to unload it, develop the negatives, and make prints.

Mr. Newsman was pleased and paid me when he picked them up. This happened several more times, always on a rush-overnight schedule. Instead of picking the pictures up, he had me bring them to his office. He came by and paid later.

The last film pack he delivered did not have a happy outcome. Mr. Newsman called late one evening as usual with his urgent request for pictures in the morning. When he delivered the film pack I could smell alcohol that lingered as he staggered back to his car. By midnight his pictures were being washed in the sink. They were pictures of a grand social event. People were formally dressed, holding glasses, and all their faces seemed to look half asleep or stupid.

Mr. Newsman obviously had over-sampled the liquid refreshment before aiming his camera at anyone. By the time he told his victims to "Sch-m-i-i-l-l-e.." he could have used someone to help him remain vertical because many pictures were taken with the room tipped twenty degrees from horizontal. Most pictures were badly framed and heads ware partly or fully cut off. Some pictures were blurred from camera motion. Not only were heads cut off, but one man in a tux stood next to a woman in a cocktail dress with his arm around her in a death grip, judging from the painful expression on the half of her face which was not cut off. A group photo was a disaster with his fingers in front of the lens covering all faces. I dried the pictures and delivered them the next morning.

Several days passed and Mr. Newsman did not drop off the payment. After several weeks, I went to his office to ask for it and his assistant said to come back. When I went again, the assistant said that Mr. Newsman felt he shouldn't have to pay for the pictures since they were so bad. It was as if he blamed me for the quality of his pictures—like I should have been able to correct all his drunken mistakes. I argued that he was the one who took the pictures and messed them up, not me. I could only develop what he had recorded on film. Developing the pictures is what I did for pay. The assistant said that he still wasn't going to pay. He got tough and threatening, so I left. I wondered, "What should I do now?" I never heard from Mr. Newsman again.

I wish I had left it there. That experience showed me some people don't play fair. You can't find a referee to force them to play fair. You don't sue a small-town newspaper for $6.00. I think I lost some energy and sleep dwelling on the cigar-puffing man who had cheated me. He muffed his photos and blamed me! That's wrong! I admire people who have been wronged, but refuse to go down to the gutter and fight to get even. They live on high ground and don't let the cheaters, slanderers, liars, and schemers rob them of their joy and happiness.

They expect to get bruised sometimes, but let the bruises heal without street fighting. They are living examples of the admonition from The Sermon on the Mount:

> **You have heard that it was said, 'An eye for an eye and a tooth for a tooth.' But I tell you not to resist an evil person. But whoever slaps you on your right cheek, turn the other to him also. If anyone wants to sue you and take away your tunic, let him have your cloak also, (Matthew 18-20)**

Looking back, I could have written a gentle letter to the Mr. Newsman mentioning that I was sorry he was unhappy with the pictures, but urging him to look at the negatives. He would see that *he* had cut off heads and people with his camera. I had printed exactly what *he* had taken with his speed-graphic camera! So the bad pictures were not my fault. I tried to do a good job for him with what he gave me to work with, but there was no way I could fix *his* damage. To be fair, he should consider doing the right thing and still pay me for my work, like he did other times. If he realized the errors were his fault, he might. If not, I'd lose for good and forget it. It might have been a good character-builder. But I never wrote that letter.

> Did someone ever knowingly cheat you and fail to correct your loss? What did you do about it? If it happened today, would you respond differently? Would God be involved in your reaction or would you feel compelled to take action to stop the person from cheating someone else?

CHAPTER 10

FAMILY FUN NIGHT

The doorbell rang and I raced downstairs to join my Friday night pals, Bob and Stan. We walked downtown to see a double feature—something we did almost every Friday when there wasn't a basketball game at our high school. We could go to the Tomahawk Club, a hangout for teens to go with or without dates for dancing, snacks, and socializing. We didn't have girl-friends and movies didn't require social skills, which we lacked at the time. We had our pick of cowboys and Indians, war stories, Sherlock Holmes, Tarzan, Robin Hood, Abbott and Costello, and once in a while a horror flick like Frankenstein or Dracula. We picked one of the four theaters, bought tickets and went in. The shows were continuous from opening time to closing with no intermissions. We watched newsreels, cartoons, and the main film, followed by a second one if a double feature was playing. You could enter at any time and stay as long as you wanted until the theater closed, or until the show reached the point where you came in. We stayed through the newsreel and cartoon, usually Bugs Bunny. If one feature was especially good, we might stay and watch it again.

    We usually ended up in my room after the movies. None of us had TVs, and cell phones were not invented yet. Consequently, we talked to each other! We also found additional distractions like picking cartoons from my huge collection of store-bought 16 mm movies and showing them on my projector. Sometimes we cut, glued, and assembled model airplanes from gift boxes people had given me. The most hilarious activity was taking snapshots of our faces, developing the negatives, and rumpling the photographic paper when we made enlargements so that our portraits were horribly distorted. Bob and Stan's faces won the prize for the most grotesque. They went home to show off their masterpieces, at the risk of their parents forbidding them to associate with me again, the kid with the twisted mind!

It was easy to get lost at my drafting table when I was alone, painting imaginary scenes where I dreamed of living someday—sprawling green hills, huge oak trees with leafy branches, distant mountains, a blue sky and soft white clouds. It was scenery I designed just for me. I could feel the warm sunshine and pleasant breeze. Any disagreeable things were excluded. The reality was that if I dared to lie down on the green grass, I would be bitten, scratched, and stung. My imagination had to eliminate flies, mosquitoes, fleas and ticks, thorns, or anything that would contribute to the misery. My painted scenery could not exist outside my imagination.

Grandma used to take me to Sunday school where I heard this from Genesis:

Then to Adam He (God) said, "Because you have heeded the voice of your wife, and have eaten from the tree which I commanded you, saying, 'You shall not eat of it', Cursed is the ground for your sake; In toil you shall eat of it all the days of your life. Both thorns and thistles it shall bring forth for you. And you shall eat the herb of the field. In the sweat of your face you shall eat bread till you return to the ground, for out of it you were taken; For dust you are, and to dust you shall return." (Genesis 3:17-19)

"That could not have been a happy occasion," I thought. When Adam and Eve ate the forbidden fruit, their Paradise was put under a curse. They also must be responsible for the countless biting bugs that prowl in the lush green pastures. One day, when God purges all that and restores this planet, removing the curse, we should be able to do like Psalm 23,

He makes me to lie down in green pastures; (Psalm 23:2a)

If I could lie down in the green, lush grass in one of my wishful landscapes, I wouldn't itch and scratch like crazy when I got up! I can let my imagination make its own rules when I dream.

A year passed and Bob, Stan, and I never got back into our Friday night routine. However, I'll always remember one Friday night that permanently affected my life for the better. Late that afternoon another friend, John, and I were dribbling basketballs and taking practice shots in his driveway when his dad drove in. After Mr. B. parked in the garage he came over and said, "Fred. how about coming back after dinner and joining us for our 'Family Fun Night?' We play games, Mrs. B. fixes snacks and root beer floats, and we have fun. I think you'll enjoy it." I thanked him and told him I would come back.

I joined John, his younger brother, and Mr. and Mrs. B. in their basement. We all played several matches of ping pong! None of us were experts, and there was always someone to chase the ball. Lots of laughter! We went upstairs and played Old Maid, where you didn't have to think too hard. More laughter! More fun! Mrs. B. kept the snacks and drinks coming. We lounged in a cozy living room as they got out a scrapbook and relived their summer vacation. I felt like they were taking me along with them! More snacks. It was suddenly late and time to ride my bike home—you could do that without fear in those days.

While pedaling to my house I could feel that something was different inside me—I was not the same as when I had come over earlier. I had experienced what a family is together! This was new! There was love, laughter, acceptance, comfort, security, assurance, belonging—all the things we crave inside, but sometimes never tell anyone. It's an inner longing that we try to hide unless someone like Mr. B. comes along and invites us over. John's family let me be part of their special family time for a little while! It was something that some people never experience. I thought, "If I ever have a family, I want us to do that—Family Fun Night.

When a new thing happens inside you, it's natural to ask yourself, "What Should I Do Now?" I felt I had to do something rather than wait for years to put this new activity to work in my own family if I ever had one. But wait! I did have a family! At that time I had a family of my own—Mom, my younger sister, and Grandma. I recall suggesting that we try having a "Fun Night" together where we could play table games and have snacks, and maybe listen to a storyteller on some of the many record albums I had. These were 78 rpm records, usually three in a set that you played on both sides to get a full story, but it worked. We were together, and it was memorable. Each of us enjoyed the bonding that came from our occasional "Family Fun Night." Thank you, Mr. B.

Having a family of my own and a "Fun Night" was still a dream, much like my imagining to lie down on the soft grass under the blue sky of the scene I had painted. I hadn't met Phyllis at the time—the young woman who one day would be the mother of our four sons. She's the one who eventually fixed snacks while all of us had fun laughing and enjoying each other at our version of Family Fun Night**.** Those nights usually ended by my telling a story in the living room with a fire in the fireplace as our sons crowded together with Mom on the couch. Now they are grown and have their own families, but they still speak about those nights together.

This was one picture of "Family Fun Night**,**" and many other pictures exist, including the gathering of single-parent families, or adoptive families, or grandparents, or aunts and uncles. In one sense, Bob, Stan, and I were a blurry "family," enjoying each other's company. If we had snacks, they were store-bought, because none of us knew how to make anything edible.

I could tell that our family nights were accomplishing something positive because our sons often invited their friends to join us. "We play games, have snacks, and have fun. You'll like it!" Their friends came and joined in the fun. None of our sons ever complained about Fridays. They often asked, "Are we having 'Fun Night' this Friday?" I know we made our share of mistakes, but this was one activity where I think we hit gold.

...He sets the poor on high, far from affliction, and makes their families like a flock. The righteous see it and rejoice, and all iniquity

stops its mouth. Whoever is wise will observe these things, and they will understand the lovingkindness of the Lord.
   (Psalms 107:41-43)

> Some families rarely enjoy close bonding experiences. Get-togethers on holidays may offer opportunities for snacks, games, visiting, and laughter. But the "Family Fun Nite" tradition left a closer mark on both the young and older family members that has lasted. Why do you think that is?

IMPRESSIONABLE YEARS

CHAPTER 11

HERO TO ZERO

A corporate story that has survived many years tells of a night watchman who made a frantic visit to the CEO's office one morning. Shaking, he said, "I hope you don't think I'm crazy, but please don't go on your business trip today." The boss asked why? "Last night on my shift I dreamed that your plane crashed with no survivors. I had to warn you." The boss thanked him, and the watchman left his office. The boss thought about it, and although he was doubtful, he decided to reschedule his flight for the next day. In the afternoon he learned that the same plane he would have taken had crashed with no survivors! He immediately called the night watchman at home, asking him to come to the office where he thanked him, rewarded him with a substantial check, and then fired him! When the CEO was asked why he had fired the man, he said that a night watchman must not sleep while on duty. *In a sense, the night watchman was a winner, but he was also a loser.*

The week before Christmas vacation my junior year, we had an all-school pep-rally in the gymnasium. One item on the agenda was the announcement of next year's football captain, who was secretly chosen by the current varsity football team. They announced my name, and the student body cheered. I remember a numb feeling with no emotions whatever. Several football players around me shouted things like, "Way to go, Fred!" "Good goin!" "Win! Win!" They slapped me on the back, shook my hand, and the key player who I had expected to be chosen said to me, "They couldn't have made a better choice!"

I enjoyed my unexpected status through the winter and summer months. August arrived and football practice began under Head Coach Z, one of the best, who led many of his teams to Big Eight Championships.

We determined to be champs again, and began to look like a well-oiled, synchronized machine in practice.

School classes started in September. One of the first things we noticed in the hallways was a new girl named Helen who had transferred from Chicago. She was different, wearing high heels instead of flats, carrying a shoulder-strap purse, and she smoked cigarettes! She stood out from the ordinary girls we knew. I learned that her parents could not handle her, so they sent her to live with an aunt and uncle in Aurora. Now she was a student at West High.

I was not girl-smart. That is, I could not tell how a girl felt by what she said or did. Helen began showing up close to me on many occasions. She sat next to me for meetings in the auditorium, at lunch in the cafeteria, and at pep rallies. I was a monitor who stood on a stairway landing between classes to caution students who ran up or down the stairs. Helen came down the same stairway on a regular basis and stopped like she was a self-appointed deputy to stand by me.

One day she asked if I could paint ceilings. Her uncle was painting his living room. Could I help him? I took the bait and went to her uncle's house. I met him and her aunt, and rolled paint onto the ceiling. Her aunt made sandwiches. Later they disappeared leaving Helen and me alone in front of the TV. Helen was kittenish and snuggled, but I panicked. My Uncle Chuck had not given me his street version of how to snuggle with girls. I was scared to the point where I suddenly remembered that I had chores waiting and rode my bike home. But she didn't give up.

There was a serious problem. Our team was losing games! We lost the first game to a weak team. For some unknown reason, the coach took me out of the lineup and put Dick in my place as a running back! I spent most game time on the bench, hardly getting to play at all after that! I was a fast runner made for the backfield. Dick lost yards, fumbled, and made no contribution to the offense. The team asked me why Coach Z played Dick instead of me. I said I did not know. "What Should I

Do Now?" I visited the coach twice at his home. He said Dick did better in a game (which was a boldface lie) and I did better in practice (which was true). I learned later from teammates that Dick's dad, a contractor, was remodeling Coach Z's house. It was after the football season that I understood why Coach Z let Dick play on the first-string team in my place since we both played the same position.

Before the last game, the big East-West Game, there was a pep rally in the gym. The cheerleaders and girlfriends of the players wore jerseys with each player's number. They lined up in football formation and pretended to run touchdown plays with an announcer chattering about the touchdown and our team winning. Then he noted that on one side of the gym was Helen with my jersey standing next to the coach. The announcer bellowed, "...and Captain Moody is discussing plays with Coach Z on the sidelines." That was humiliating. Everyone knew I was captain and that Coach Z didn't put me in the games. I wanted to cry. I wished I was dead. I detested Coach Z. We lost the big game. We only won one game that year!

The Christmas Dance in December was one where the girls asked the guys. I hoped at one time that Helen would ask me to escort her, but after the football season and my status drop from hero to zero, she avoided me. I learned she had asked someone else. Several weeks passed and most of my friends had dates. I definitely was a loser! A big zero! I could only hope that, "Maybe 10 or 20 years from now it won't hurt so much." I had no answer to the question, "What should I do now?"

It was a gloomy, cold Saturday afternoon in November when the phone rang. A girl's voice said, "You don't know me—I'm Phyllis Ivemeyer. If you don't already have plans would you care to escort me to the Christmas Dance?" This was another blank moment like the one after they announced my name as football captain. I couldn't believe I was experiencing such a similar shock, bundled with joy and the realization that I am a loser but someone out there has not checked out my dismal background sheet! She can't possibly know she is talking to a

ZERO! The only words that came were, "Uh, when is it?" I knew when it was. She told me the date. I asked if I could call her back after I checked to see if I was going to be in town or not. I hurried to look up her picture in our previous yearbook. Then I called her right back. "Thank you! I will be glad to escort you." That phone call slowly developed into a friendship so deep that we almost made it to our 59th wedding anniversary. Phyllis was not afraid to take a chance on someone who was a zero! God gave us a precious life together until she passed quietly from cancer into the arms of her Savior.

What about my feelings for Coach Z? I should thank him for making my life miserable during that football season. The pain, humiliation, and suffering of those few months were small compared to the lifetime of joy and happiness that came after one phone call. It had to be a real-life example of...

...we know that all things work together for good to those who love God, to those who are the called according to His purpose. (Romans 8:28)

> Did your world "fall apart" at some time? Something happened and then life was one miserable hour after another. Your misery clouded any bright future you once had and life did not seem worth living. I know the feeling. Some people hurting like that turn to drugs and drink to induce a stupor where all pain vanishes for a time, but the cause of pain remains. But some have discovered that God really loves them, cares for them and the scripture above is true—but we need to believe it to experience its reality. Can you agree with that and tell your story?

CHAPTER 12

CHOICES?

The boss asked me for a quick estimate of a vessel decompression time as we passed in the hallway. I didn't realize that he would immediately send my estimate to the customer as if it was the final word. He trusted me. But I discovered later that the quick estimate might be wrong. "What Shall I Do Now?" I had to make a choice: Tell the boss, and he would suffer embarrassment with the customer; or I could do a detailed analysis which would take all day, and all night too, and hope that my quick estimate was reasonable. It turned out that my estimate of decompression time was accurate. (Whew!) Doing the analysis was a good choice.

Another time, I traveled to a national convention to receive the George Westinghouse Heat Transfer Award. The award chairman told me by phone that I should give a 10-minute acceptance speech. Following lunch and cocktails prior to receiving the award, I told the half-drunk president of the society that I was asked to give an acceptance speech. He told me not to do it, but just to shake his hand and sit down. "What Shall I Do Now?" I had to choose whether to follow the instructions of the award chairman, or the president, who reeked of alcohol and obviously wanted to keep control of center stage. That is, I had to either sit down and stay silent or speak.

When the president handed me the award, paused for the flash bulb, and loosened his sweaty hand from mine, I turned to the lectern and faced over 300 attendees. I made the choice and gave my acceptance speech. The president was scowling alongside me, but the crowd was responsive. They cheered. Immediately after the speech, before the president could say a word, I hurried to the exit, took an airport taxi, and headed for home. Later, many letters came expressing appreciation for the speech.

Not all my choices have worked out well. A friend of the family urged us to invest generously in limited partnerships some years ago. His high enthusiasm about how people would increase their lifetime savings, lured dozens of his friends, including us, to invest with him. The entire partnership fizzled. His partner disappeared with the majority of investments. Bad choice.

Therefore, making a choice can be risky!

The risk of making a choice may be why some people are afraid of making commitments, because commitments include choices.

Fear of making commitments may lead to missed opportunities.

During my pre-teen years, making choices was not too consequential. The stakes usually were not high. Choosing was more like a dart board game. Throw the dart and follow the instructions. Life was simple then.

But I learned that things change with time. Making choices became much more than a dart board game during my high school years. The consequences of my choices were bigger. Making choices was no longer a game. Now, more often, I was *forced* to make choices.

I needed money to do the things I wanted to do. The little money Mom could pay me for odd jobs wasn't enough. She worked hard at her job to support us. I couldn't ask her for more. To earn money, I had two prospects:

1. I could get a job to earn money for the things I wanted.
2. I could start a business of my own and earn money that way.

"What Should I Do Now?" It was my last few months before high school graduation and I knew I had to start making important choices in my life. Some choices were easy: Which movie to see? Miniature golfing or the zoo? A malted milk or a chocolate Sundae? But other choices that called for a serious commitment scared me. If I applied for a job, I would have to answer to a boss and follow rules, and my life would not be free as it was now. I might sign up to be a "slave" without realizing there would be no way to gain back my freedom! I couldn't tell in advance if my choice would be good or bad. I could imagine successes or consequences, based on my limited experience and what others said, but the outcome was not guaranteed.

If I got a job, someone would pay me, but they'd also tell me what I had to do. I liked my independence, doing things my own way, at my own pace, when I wanted to. When I cut grass or shoveled snow for older ladies, I was my own boss—but those jobs didn't pay enough. Besides, the grass didn't grow fast enough to keep me busy. Neither did it snow so I could shovel sidewalks in the summer months. One morning I woke up with a great idea! I could start my own business developing films and printing pictures for people overnight using the darkroom kit Mom had given me for Christmas! I hurried to make posters with attached snapshot samples of kids, families, and pets, with bargain prices listed which were ten-percent of drugstore prices!

Neighborhood grocery stores placed my poster on their checkout counters. I got one order in a month and collected 35 cents for developing one roll of film with pictures. I think that most people would not take a roll of film that contained irreplaceable shots of a family vacation, wedding, reunion, or other special occasion, and entrust it to a neighborhood teenager who might lose it or otherwise mess up the negatives and lose the precious shots forever, when they could be assured of a good set of prints from a drug-store. "What Should I Do Now?"

I decided that earning money was more important than the method (although some methods were on the "No" list, like "robbing stores" or devising "counterfeit currency). The method of earning it was no longer important, as long as it was legal and proper. Therefore, I would get a job as a "hired slave" and suffer through a few hours of bondage during the week, performing whatever the boss said to do. I had already done that in school whenever a teacher demanded us to do a difficult homework. The sacrifice in working at a job for someone else would be minor if it meant getting a pay envelope each week with a few dollars in it.

I learned that you can change your mind about what you are willing to do when you discover either (1) the best you can do by yourself is rejected, or (2) what you can do by yourself has limitations.

Maybe I couldn't sell my film developing because I lacked marketing skills. Perhaps I should have made small flyers and distributed them door-to-door, but that would be too much like trying to sell magazines, which I had failed in elementary school. I decided I should look at want-ads and choose one. If it didn't work, I'd try the next.

It wasn't hard to find jobs where I didn't need special skills. If I could use a shovel, broom, trash can, and follow simple instructions, most places would hire me. Maybe I wouldn't get a very exotic job, but it would provide some folding cash. That was the upside of several employers I worked for. However, I learned some valuable life lessons from the downsides of those employers.

One Proverb stands out that I adopted for when I have to make an important choice:

Trust in the Lord with all your heart, and lean not on your own understanding; In all your ways acknowledge Him, and He shall direct your paths. (Proverbs 3:5,6)

There is also a reassuring promise God made to His People, which shows His care for them when they call on Him for help and guidance in making choices:

For I know the thoughts that I think toward you, says the Lord, thoughts of peace and not of evil, to give you a future and a hope.

Then you will call upon Me and go and pray to Me, and I will listen to you. And you will seek Me and find Me, when you search for Me with all your heart. **(Jeremiah 29: 11-13)**

> Suppose you have to make a choice and you are going to be interviewed. You have to answer questions about why you made that choice. Have you ever had to explain in great detail why you made a certain choice? What principles guided you in making the choice? Worldly? Biblical? Philosophical?

CHAPTER 13

DIRTY MACHINE SHOP

I was on my bike looking for any job when I saw the sign, *HABERLE ENGINEERING.* Mr. Haberle was sitting at the only desk and motioned for me to come in when I opened the door to ask about a job. He knew I could only be there for one reason and he didn't say a word. He just puffed on a cigar and studied my physique. He gave me hiring papers to fill out and took me into the machine shop. Amidst the noise of machines and the smell of oil, he introduced me to a foreman. "Emil will get you started." Then Mr. Haberle hurried back to his office.

Emil was a good-natured foreman who first showed me how to attach gears to Jeep drive shafts. One gurney contained steel shafts like short broom sticks; the other gurney contained gears. I set a gear in a holder, put one end of a shaft into it, and pulled a lever to press them together. It was an easy, boring, but a paying job. After an hour, I was aware of someone standing behind me. Mr. Haberle was counting each drive I assembled with a stopwatch. Then he pushed me aside and showed how to *grab-place-pull-toss, grab-place-pull-toss,* one after the other at lightning speed, telling me I could do it five times faster! I tried, but I had to think. He smiled, nodded approval, and went away. I did not resent Mr. Haberle pushing me to work faster. After all, he gave me a job. I could at least do my best to make him happy that he took a chance on me. I actually felt good later that day when I noticed the other gurney almost filled up with my assembled drive shafts!

A few days later when I came to work, someone called, "Hey, Fred!" It was Bob G., a kid about my age who had been hired a week earlier. I hardly knew him because we went to different schools. We talked for a minute, and then he lowered his voice. "I've found the perfect place to hide out! You can spend hours there and nobody will find you!" I couldn't believe what he was telling me. He looked around. "C'mon, I'll show you." He wanted to show me a hideout where he could spend hours to avoid working! My common sense psychoanalysis told me, *this kid has a problem!* I told him, "No thanks. I think I would rather work. It makes the time go faster." That ended the conversation.

If I had to hide out in a lonely room by myself, it would be agonizing! With only myself as company??? With nothing to do??? Even a few cockroaches would be welcome guests! A spider in the corner would help. I could even become friends with a rat! But being alone in a small room? How could Bob stand to be with only himself for several hours—no conversation, no adventure, no excitement—only burps and farts—his own, or other body sounds—you know? I think he would go crazy! But he was proud that he had found a hideout! My semi-professional opinion is that Bob had a *fractured viewpoint*. Maybe a bad childhood experience, or he got dropped on his head, but his viewpoint definitely was *fractured*.

Bob was cheating his employer by hiding out, and he was also cheating himself because he could have seen things in the shop which might have given him a new vision for his *fractured* viewpoint. For example, I saw machines doing impossible things! How could a machine made out of metal be used to cut another solid piece of metal? I saw a solid steel tube as big as a stovepipe rotating on one machine while a cutting tool made a deep groove in it. Long steel ribbons peeled off at the cutting blade and curled onto the floor. A perfect design was being cut on the cylinder's surface! Another machine was stretching a metal shaft like a piece of taffy. In another process, a chunk of metal was heated to glowing white, and pressed into a perfect shape. What I saw in that and other machine shops opened up new visions for me.

Metal filings, strands, and chips accumulated on the floor around many of the machines. These had to be removed regularly—a job nobody wanted. That job fell to me and I determined to make each workspace sparkle because I knew that the machinists needed a clean floor to stand on as they operated their machines. They noticed the clean, dry floor spaces with some surprise and gratitude. It was rewarding—almost like the old ladies whose grass I had cut years ago.

I needed to earn money. That drove me to find a job. I didn't need special skills, but the dirty machine shop was one environment that stretched my view of the world in a positive way. And that was just the beginning!

> A highly esteemed manager of mine once told an all-employee meeting, "If you want to succeed in your job, dedicate yourself to making your boss a success. You may not like him, or approve of his methods, but if you work to make him succeed in his mission, word gets around and soon, everyone wants you. That is how you can succeed. Make the boss a success." In one sense I was helping to make Mr. Haberle successful in meeting his quota because he took a chance on me by giving me a job.

Servants, do what you're told by your earthly masters. And don't just do the minimum that will get you by. Do your best. Work from the heart for your real Master, for God, confident that you'll get paid in full when you come into your inheritance. Keep in mind always that the ultimate master you're serving is Christ. The sullen servant who does shoddy work will be held responsible. Being Christian doesn't cover up bad work. (Colossians 3:22-25, "The Message")

> Have you had to work at a job where you could not use your full potential or abilities? Did you have a choice other than "job or no job?" What did you do about it? Was there a point of view that changed the job from highly disagreeable to something more fulfilling? If so, was it Solomon's wisdom, believing that it was part of God's plan for you, or just fate? Others including me want to learn what happened.

CHAPTER 14

FEET AND FLUOROSCOPE

School started in September and my job ended at the machine shop that did not employ part-time workers. I heard about a shoe store that needed extra help. The sun didn't set before I visited *R & S Shoes*.

The interview was short with the boss; a big, loud Italian. My only shoe experience was tying my own shoes and watching the town blacksmith heat, hammer, and nail iron shoes on horses. "Can you tie shoes on someone sitting in front of you?" Sure! "You're hired!"

I learned where the shoes were stacked in the back room, and caught on quickly. It was a God-given education that would come in handy later because I learned brand names like Buster Brown, Converse, Keds, and a few popular names at the time. The routine was simple. A customer comes in and looks at all the shoes on display, or they sit down and say they need a new pair. If they are vague, you take over and bring out the most expensive pair, slip one on their foot, check appearance in a floor mirror, and "Oooh and Aaah!" over how good it looks on them You slip the other shoe on and check the fit as you have the customer step onto the fluoroscope viewer. Their feet and toe bones show inside the shoe outlines while they admire the greenish transparent foot and shoe images. You hold down the switch, giving them a big dose of radiation, which increases their probability of cancer. It's free and helps make sales. (The danger of x-rays was not known at that time.)

There were times when a customer had two different sized feet and a pair of shoes from one box did not work. I would ask myself, "What Should I Do Now?" That's when the boss came to the rescue. I think he sold the size for the larger foot and put stuffing into the other shoe for the smaller foot.

I panicked when a customer had only one leg or one leg in a cast that covered one foot. Why not take two boxes of identical shoes and mix them with two right shoes in one box and two left shoes in the other. Then I could sell a pair of two right or two left shoes, depending on which leg the customer still had, and save the other box for a future customer with the opposite remaining leg, hoping the foot size I saved would fit. After careful thought, I concluded it was not a good idea, so I called the boss for assistance while I tried to find a different customer to help. I never learned how the boss solved those problems.

Men usually bought the first or second pair, but women often wanted a shoe at least two sizes too small! Even if their foot almost burst the straps and turned blue by strangulation, they would sigh, "That's puurrfect! Wrap it up!" The driving force must have been self-image, thinking they had a tiny foot. Their mental attitude must have numbed their pain. If it was my shoe store, I would have those women sign a disclaimer releasing us from medical disasters caused by cutting off blood flow to the feet, leading to amputation.

I liked working for my Italian boss. He had a great sense of humor and was not hard to please. He gave me good pointers on how to respond to difficult customers, and when to let them alone. He often told funny stories from his Italian background, and an occasional joke most Italians would understand, but they were over my head so I laughed to be polite. The shoe store was an enjoyable education for me. The Bible says of servants,

...*Whatsoever you do, do it heartily as to the Lord and not to men.* (Colossians 3:23)

The *heartily* part was easy to follow although I knew very little about the Bible at the time.

Homework projects took more time than I expected, so my hours selling shoes dwindled. It was a good thing because I learned things I wish I could have ignored. The boss was married and his wife managed the cash register. He was a playful gentleman, jovial with customers, kind to me, but he had a shady side. I couldn't help overhear his conversations on the backroom phone when I was replacing shoeboxes. He made plans for his buddies to meet Saturday night in one of their homes for a beer fest and a hot porno movie that the pharmacist would bring. I could hardly believe my ears! My boss planned a drinking party with his buddies to watch porno movies! It gave me a sick feeling. I felt even sicker because the pharmacist he mentioned was another man I knew and respected, and he was providing the porno flick! He was a fine man well-known for his charitable work on city organizations. He also took a special interest in me and my photography hobby. He gave me helpful advice about the photographic paper he sold me for enlargements, and he told me which chemical developers to use for film and prints. But on this fateful day, two of my male idols fell off their pedestals.

That had a destructive effect on me that made me wonder "What should I do now?" I had to do something because every time I saw or heard the boss, it reminded me of his back-room phone conversations. Going to the shoe store was no longer fun. Fortunately, school projects demanded more time and my hours at the shoe store were almost squeezed to zero. I told the boss I better "take a leave." He agreed, and being able to avoid the shoe store helped me get back "on track." At that stage of my life, I was not ready to confront an adult about his appetite for "porno flicks." As I grew older, I could have asked a question like, "I'm trying to understand why people are drawn to pornography. What is the attraction for you?" But I wasn't ready for any such conversation then. I think the best solution for me at that time of my life was to avoid reminders. But I did miss the weekly pay.

A girl in my Latin class knew I had sold shoes. Her parents owned a smaller shoe store and they needed help on Saturdays. Would I consider? I was glad to help her parents by carrying shoe deliveries downstairs for them to stock shelves. They paid generously. They also asked me to wait on customers when it got busy. I recall one businessman who wanted an expensive pair of wing tip shoes. I unboxed the most expensive brand. He was happy with the first pair he tried on. I asked him, "Are you sure they're OK?" The owners were observing me, and almost went apoplectic because I didn't instantly ring up the sale. He insisted they were OK and I casually made the sale. Afterwards, they told me, "Never, never do that! When a customer says he's satisfied, rush to the cash register!" I think they were telling me the old proverb, "A bird in the hand is worth two in the bush."

They were a sweet, Jewish couple with high morals. It was a delight to work for them, and their high work ethic had many features I decided to practice if I ever ran a company—honesty, integrity, generosity, sensitivity, orderliness, and trust. When you spend time working for people like that, it leaves a deep mark on you!

When wisdom enters your heart, and knowledge is pleasant to your soul, discretion will preserve you; understanding will keep you, to deliver you from the way of evil, from the man who speaks perverse things, from those who leave the paths of uprightness to walk in the ways of darkness; who rejoice in doing evil, and delight in the perversity of the wicked; (Proverbs 1:10-14)

> No doubt you already have and will continue to encounter people who give you good, questionable, and bad examples of character. Think of one person you have admired for their good character. What positive impression have they made on you? How did they do that? Can you identify opportunities you have to make a positive impression on someone else? How can you avoid making a questionable or bad impression?

CHAPTER 15

CONSTRUCTION WORKER

"How come Homer don't like you?" One of the carpenters at the construction site of the new West High School building had pulled me aside because he had seen how the labor foreman treated me. "I don't know," I mumbled back. I had just graduated two weeks before and started this summer job before heading to college in the fall. I was hired as a common laborer by Mr. Leis, the owner of the construction company.

My first assignment: Homer told me to take a shovel and wheelbarrow and spread gravel from a nearby pile over a floor area. The first three hours were easy, and then it was lunchtime. Rats had eaten my lunch that day, which was in a paper bag! One of the men shared his chips, but after that I brought my lunch in a metal box.

I had finished spreading gravel when Homer came yelling, "That's too high! We gotta pour concrete over it—there's no room for concrete! How dumb can you get?" I told him he hadn't said how high, and I couldn't read his mind. He mumbled something about how I should have known if I used my head. Then he said to one of the nearby workers, "Don't ask Mr. College Man here to do anything—he's too stupid!" Welcome to the first week!

Homer had me scrape concrete forms, carry loads of bricks, and do lots of odd jobs, always referring to me with a sneer as, "Mr. College Man!" Nothing I did was ever right. Homer always yelled about something being wrong. It was obvious to other workers that he took a personal dislike to me, but I still got paid. The other workers were friendly. I wondered why Homer took such a dislike to me. He was cozy with all the other men, treating them like good friends. Maybe he just needed someone to bully who could not fight back. By diminishing one person he could raise his own self-image. I could last.

About the third week, Mr. Leis came on site and called everyone together. The union had planned a strike, but he promised to raise the hourly rate if his workers would not strike. Also, he said that he had enough work lined up for everyone for the next six years. "Stick with Arnie and you won't get laid off! You'll have a steady job for at least six more years!" You could hear sighs of relief and approval from the workers. That afternoon a dozen or more regular workers and I got layoff notices and a final check! Mr. Leis was nowhere in sight to answer anyone's questions. (That's when I stopped believing in the Easter Bunny!) "What Should I Do Now?"

This was a *first* for me! A high class businessman, owner of the construction company that had the general contract for building the new high school, had personally promised that he would not lay anyone off. But he did! If you can't trust the top boss, who can you trust?

Lying lips are an abomination to the Lord, but those who deal truthfully are His delight. (Proverbs 12:22)

Kids learn from their role models; they choose qualities they want to imitate because they admire them. They also choose qualities they want to avoid, because they portray hypocrisy, weakness, and, topping the list*, untrustworthiness*. That would describe why I would not want to imitate Mr. Leis. What about Homer?

A few weeks later, I saw Homer get shoved out of a bar, followed by a huge, muscular woman, who turned out to be his wife. She was at least one head taller and I think 100 pounds heavier than Homer. She grabbed his arm in a vice grip and marched him along like a puppy dog. I said, "Hi, Homer," as we passed, walking in opposite directions. He glared at me while she jerked him on.

***Whoever rewards evil for good, evil will not depart from his house.* (Proverbs 17:13)**

But I still had to find another summer job.

******

That was the last time I saw Homer. The new West High School was finished in several more years, but by then, Phyllis (the girl I met as a high school senior) and I were married and settled in California. After 59 years together and a family of four sons plus their families, Phyllis died. Twelve years later I had a yearning to visit our home town, Aurora, Illinois. My four sons, two of their wives, and two grandkids wanted to go along, so last year we made the trip. We visited the new West High School on our itinerary.

What used to be 850 students when I graduated was now 3500 and tops in national STEM (Science, Technology, Engineering, and Mathematics). I had written the current principal, noting how West High had launched me to a fulfilling career in technology. He gave us a four-hour escorted tour through the buildings and grounds where I had dumped pea-gravel for some floors and carried bricks for walls many years ago. Memories!

> Did you ever work for a boss who found fault with everything you did? He/she micromanaged, watching for your slightest misstep? If that describes one of your bosses, how did you survive? You have dozens of eager people struggling in the same way that need to hear from you. Explain how you got through it. Did you revolt? Fight? Pray? Quit? What?

CHAPTER 16

MAIL CARRIER

My mom gave me a 1940 Chevy for a high school graduation present in 1953. It was a trade-in at the automobile agency where she was office manager. They told her the single owner was an elderly woman who only drove it to the store. She didn't say which store—it burned oil and had over a hundred thousand miles on it! It ran well and now I was driving it as I searched for another job. When I passed the post office, I thought it would be a waste of time, but I parked at the front entrance anyway and went inside.

Mailmen with letter bags were walking out as I found my way to the postmaster's office. The man at a desk, Mac, said the carriers needed extra help to carry their routes while they took summer vacations. I had to pay fifty cents to get bonded. Rules were strict. Never put a stamp on an unstamped envelope—put it in the *return to sender* box. If postage was due on an item, don't leave it without collecting the money, even if it was just a few cents! I should leave a note with the option for the addressee to leave the money in their mailbox for the carrier. Government rules were rigid, threatening, and a few were absurd (I thought) in those days.

Each carrier had a desk at the post office with an open cupboard of 300 to 400 slots, one for each addressee on his route. I helped put mail into the slots for the route I would help carry each day. There were envelopes, newspapers, and magazines to roll up. Walking fast, it took two to three hours to deliver a route. Ed, the carrier boss told me, "Don't come back before 3:00 PM. The carriers spend time visiting with their customers. You won't do much visiting because you don't know them, so you will finish early. Go home and have a long lunch so you don't make the other carriers look bad." I did as he told me, usually having two hours to spend at home. I would get back to the post office as the other carriers were returning. It was a tiring job with lots of walking, but it was outdoors and the pay was good.

The only dangers were trying to avoid becoming a lightning rod during occasional thundershowers, and watching out for dogs. If a dog came rushing at me, I lowered my mailbag toward the animal and it backed away. One dog lived in an expensive mansion. I had never seen him, but his deep bark and snarling was cause for alarm. When I would walk on the curved driveway toward his residence, he would slam against the door. I tried pushing the mail through the slot but the beast always tore it out of my grip.

One Friday I started up the driveway and the growling began, but this time the expensive door burst open and the black and white dog headed straight toward me. I had only a rolled-up *Life* magazine for self-defense, which I swung, hitting him squarely on the forehead. He barked and ran in a circle before a return attack. I hit him again— six times! Then a woman screamed from the doorway, and the dog ran back into the house. She apologized and assured me that the dog couldn't hurt anyone because he had no teeth and was almost blind. The dog didn't tell me that—he wasn't wearing a sign or candy-stripe collar to advertise his handicap. I would have hit him anyway, but unbeknownst to me, the dog had ripped my pants in the back with a claw. When I returned to the Post Office a carrier asked me if knew my underwear was showing. Hazards of the job! That explained why some young kids on the bus were giggling at me! Someone advised me to sue the dog's owner, but I might have to wear the same outfit with the damage showing in a court of law. I neglected the advice.

There were other hazards. "Yes, I knew how to drive. Yes, my Chevy had a stick shift." That qualified me to drive one of the parcel-post trucks and deliver packages because the P. O. was short on drivers. A truck was already loaded with packages addressed to downtown stores on Broadway. No one mentioned that these deliveries should be made at the rear entrances. I climbed into the driver's seat after learning where the various controls were. The gearshift on the floor was almost like my car, on the steering wheel.

The truck I drove was at the dock. Neutral gear. Brake on. Start the engine. Clutch in. Shift to first gear, and off I drove in full control of a several thousand dollar machine belonging to the U. S. government! Easy. Second gear just like my car. Turn signals flashing –good. After navigating several blocks, I was driving down Broadway. The stores were on my right. I double- parked, picked up my first package, and walked into the store. Clerks directed me toward the back to an office where the occupant gave me a dirty look, and pointed to a place to put the package. I made similar stops at ten more stores and had one package left for a side street.

When I turned onto the side street I suddenly had a big problem: all the traffic was coming toward me, honking. I had driven half a block before figuring out they were telling me it was a one-way street! I had to back up. But where was the reverse gear? Every shift slot only resulted in forward motion! After two panicked minutes, I decided the truck did not have a reverse gear! "What Should I Do Now?" Then one calm gentleman in a convertible going the opposite direction, pulled alongside me. He must have been aware of my increasing desperation because he coached me on where to find the reverse gear and then guided me backwards out of the one-way street. (He had to be an angel!) I was too shaken to make the final delivery so I returned to the post office and left the last package for the next driver. Hopefully they would ignore me for driving ever again. But destiny did not work that way.

The next day they asked me to drive a panel truck for deliveries. It was a smaller vehicle with a shift identical to my Chevy. However, one of the rear door latches was broken and was held shut with rope. When I turned a corner, the door swung open, making a prominent gash in the front fender of a new car. The driver was hysterical! He had just picked up the car from the showroom and was taking it home to show his wife! After he quieted down, he followed me back to the post office, and took care of the insurance paperwork. Thankfully, that was my last week before starting college. I think I left before they concluded that I was a jinx" for many of the mishaps that had plagued the P. O. Aside from stumbling through various assignments, the P. O. was a great experience—for me.

Keep sound wisdom and discretion; so they will be life to your soul and grace to your neck. Then you will walk safely in your way, and your foot will not stumble. (Proverbs 21b-23)

> Every new job has a "learning curve." Does that make it more or less interesting? The Bible teaches that the Lord intends for us to keep learning *(Let the wise listen and add to their learning, and let the discerning get guidance--.* Proverbs 1:5 NIV} Describe what is happening today where you are presently learning something new. Is it pleasant? Stressful? Something you prefer to avoid?

CHAPTER 17

FIRST YEAR AT COLLEGE— BRAVE NEW WORLD

I drove my '40 Chevy 140 miles to southern Illinois, packed with enough socks, shirts, and shorts to last until Christmas break (I hoped) without having to do laundry. The car was a high school graduation gift from Mom, who had me promise not to drive over 40 mph. She read that most fatal accidents occur at higher speed.

It was not hard for me to leave home. Otherwise, I could never reach the dreams bouncing around in my head. The hard part was being away from Phyllis, my serious girlfriend. We were engaged to be engaged. I had given her a gold-plated *friendship ring* to mark our commitment to each other. She would be attending Illinois College, 60 miles from Blackburn, where I was enrolled. We had already planned weekend visits—"Thanks, Mom, for the Chevy!"

The road sign said, "Carlinville, population 2170." I rolled onto the Blackburn campus. It was several days before official opening, so I parked at Butler Hall, the men's dorm. Lugging my bulging suitcase down a hallway I heard a squeaky voice call out, "Hello. I'm Wesley. Looks like we both got here early." His parents had dumped him a few hours earlier with a long list of instructions. He helped me unpack my car. It was nice to have company, although Wesley was strange. "I have to visit Miss Jones," he said. "Come again?" I asked. He meant that he had to go to the restroom. "Oh." We ate at a local eatery, and explored the campus together. Wesley had to call home often to check in according to his mom's instructions.

When the semester started, Wesley moved to the second floor to join his pre-assigned roommate. I had two assigned roommates, Nick and Hunter, who arrived and livened up the entire dorm from our basement lair. They were country boys who knew all about growing corn. They were also experts about women—the kind who could handle six-shooters, mostly for rattlesnakes (not the two-legged kind) and barn rats. These boys were take-charge, friendly types who laughed a lot and were not afraid to offer opinions on every topic. After a few weeks they learned I was good at math and science (two things they deplored) but they respected me for that. I helped them with their math homework.

I was shocked to learn at the first all-school welcome assembly that freshmen were forbidden to bring automobiles to campus. If I had known that rule, I would have looked for another college! I did keep the car *off campus* to satisfy the rule (sort of). A grandmotherly lady in town rented her garage to me for five dollars a month. That was home for my Chevy except on weekends when I drove the 60 miles to visit Phyllis at Illinois College.

Blackburn was a co-op liberal arts college where students worked half-time for the school to help pay their tuition. Mom had saved enough to pay the excess for one year. She was the reason I went to college. Although she never went, she wanted me and my sister to have the opportunity.

Girls worked in housekeeping, the kitchen, and laundry room. Some guys worked with a construction foreman building a new dormitory. Students from the city did not know the business end of a pick or how to use a post-hole digger! The professional plumbers, electricians, and bricklayers stumbled over the students, who mostly got in the way, delaying the construction schedule.

We also rotated jobs in maintenance, trash and garbage pickup, and caring for a few farm animals which included pigs, cows, and steers, owned by the school. Occasionally we coaxed a hog into a truck for his last ride. That was emotional for some guys who had bonded with the fat beast like a pet. Similar to cars, pets were not allowed on campus either. A few days later, pork chops, bacon, and ham showed up for meals in the dining room. "Please pass a slice of Porky's back leg with a little horseradish."

My weekend funds were almost gone by Christmas, and I became anxious and depressed. This was important enough for me to gather my best problem-solving abilities together for a solution. While my brain was straining on what to do, several Blackburn students needed a ride to Chicago and gladly chipped in for gas. I drove with Phyllis and four other students in the Chevy, bulging with students and their baggage. We reached Chicago in a snowstorm sometime after midnight. I carried mail again the week before Christmas, which helped pay for a few weekend trips to see Phyllis during the second semester.

I had returned to Blackburn after Christmas with my camera and darkroom equipment. A number of love affairs had blossomed on campus and new couples wanted photos of each other. There was a good market for my 8 X 10 black and white portraits which I developed in an empty storage room. I had almost no "customers" from science and math majors. Either they had no romantic interests or they were too fascinated by paradoxes, conundrums, and mathematical puzzles to be distracted by soft music and perfume. I enjoyed math, but I lived for the weekend visits with Phyllis—and perfume.

Photographing the guys was easy. I hung up a smooth blanket, sat the guy on a stool and flash! Next! Taking the girls' photos was a pain. I had to set up in their dorm parlor under the vulture eyes of their housemother because the place was off-limits to all men—except me with a special pass signed by the dean of students, Mrs. P., who had the reputation of a prison guard. Each girl came in separately, dressed in her finest. Everything she wore had to be in place—hair, earrings, makeup, necklace, lipstick. Finally she would pose and wait while I focused and lowered the room lights to almost dark while the housemother panicked. I opened the shutter, fired the flash, closed the shutter, and turned up the room lights. Next! Everyone got their picture for a dollar. Almost 200 photos provided gasoline to visit Phyllis and take her to dinner and a movie the rest of the semester.

The pictures I took were almost professional quality, with one distinguishing feature: everyone's eyes had large, black pupils—that is, they resembled "hoot-owls." But nobody complained. I had to use the flash in the darkened room with the shutter open. (My equipment had no connection between the camera and flash.)

One time, I visited Phyllis on a cold, dark Saturday in February, feeling crummy. Rain was predicted for that night, and I knew it would be stupid to drive 60 miles back to Blackburn in a storm. Acting on the advice of my roommates, I stopped at the police station to ask if I could spend the night there rather than risk the drive. They agreed. After Phyllis and I went to a pizza parlor and movie it began to rain. By the time I checked into the police department, it was pouring. They took my coat, wallet, and belt, gave me a pillow and blanket, and escorted me to a large, empty cell which would hold about 10 prisoners. The bed space was a series of box-like shelves large enough for a man to lie down on a thin mattress. They locked the bars, and I crawled into the first box, laid my head on the pillow, and covered up with the blanket.

I ached and had a fever with slight chills, but I was asleep in a few minutes and did not wake up until morning. The aches, fever, and chills were gone. Throughout the night the room had filled up with occupants and smelled like alcohol. Several men were staring at me, mumbling something like I did not look familiar. I took that as a compliment. One of the cops escorted me out, returned my coat, wallet, and belt, and wished me "Good-day." It was cold and wet, but the rain had stopped. After brushing my teeth, combing my hair, and washing my face in cold water at a gas station, I picked up Phyllis at her college for church. Then we had lunch at a restaurant before I returned to Blackburn.

The last significant Blackburn experience I had was motivated by a favorite professor, and had nothing to do with students or academics.

My math professor became a good friend. He was aware of my family situation and during one of our coffee discussions, he suggested that I should contact my dad—just to settle in my own mind what kind of man he was. Rather than see him as the one who abandoned me, my mom and sister, making me think I was defective because he never came back—maybe I should meet him. I could have anticipated my mom's hysterics when I mentioned it, but after a few days when she came *down off the ceiling*, she agreed it was probably a good idea and she got his address from my aunt.

His first welcoming written reply was, "If you're looking for money, save your breath!" He had never given Mom any child support anyway. "No. I just wanted to meet you," I answered. He agreed. I wrote that I could even bring my own thermos of water to avoid impacting his expenses. We met at my aunt's apartment in Chicago (his sister's dwelling). It was a disappointment. Polite words, but no mention of why he left. Nothing like, "I'm sorry." It was cordial! I could have stopped a stranger on the street and had a more heartfelt discussion. About noon I met my dad's second wife (a former neighbor who had dumped her husband for my dad). He also introduced me to my half-sister—a sweet girl—a relative I never knew I had. She had to be ignorant of the ugly family affairs that preceded her. She was about the same age I was when my dad left our family.

A short visit over lunch was shallow. I kept thinking, "There was a time when this man—my dad—and I were close pals. We did things together. Now it's like we're strangers. This white-haired woman sitting at the table has succeeded in erasing all loving memory of his previous life. I wondered what she thought of me." But I remained polite.

I hurried back from this non-event to the lively world of Blackburn College. "How was your trip to Chicago, Fred?" "It was OK." They cared enough to ask! I felt deeper appreciation for my dorm friends than I ever felt before—even the obnoxious ones! The Bible says,

Bear one another's burdens, and so fulfill the law of Christ. (Galatians 6:2)

They were doing that—helping me carry emotions I tried to hide. I tried to pretend that meeting my dad was not upsetting—but it really was. I had higher expectations that had dissolved in disappointment. There was another biblical truth I did not know at the time:

> **Therefore, humble yourselves under the mighty hand of God, that He may exalt you in due time, casting all your care upon Him, for He cares for you. (I Peter 5:6,7)**

When I finally heard about that truth, it was like the start of a new day. There were times when I was disappointed and asked myself, "What Should I Do Now?" Disappointments would have been easier to handle if I was aware of another biblical message offered to believers:

> **Consider it a sheer gift, friends, when tests and challenges come at you from all sides. You know that under pressure, your faith-life is forced into the open and shows its true colors. So don't try to get out of anything prematurely. Let it do its work so you become mature and well developed, not deficient in any way. If you don't know what you're doing, pray to the Father. He loves to help. You'll get His help, and won't be condescended to when you ask for it. Ask boldly, believingly, without a second thought. (James 1:2-6a, The Message)**

The school year ended. By then I had decided to become an engineer, but Blackburn did not offer an engineering degree. Only major universities offered engineering degrees. One of the closest ones was the University of Wisconsin.

> *Was there an episode in this chapter that grabbed your attention? Did a strange man ever appear out of the shadows and announce that he was your biological father? Did you ever attempt to re-connect with an estranged parent or other family member? Was the result happy or sad? Should you take the credit or blame for the outcome? Others have been disappointed in similar ways and need to hear your story.*

CHAPTER 18

MAIL CARRIER, *DIFFERENT SHERIFF*

After one year away at college, I came home and was hired again for a summer job at the post office. Ed, the carrier boss loved by all, had retired and was replaced by Mac, who had hired me the year before. Everything was different among the carriers as they quietly shoved mail into the slots. There was no laughing, talking, or lighthearted atmosphere like the previous year. Mac was walking the aisles, not saying a word. The carriers were ignoring him. It was like a funeral parlor. I carried a route for one of the regulars who told me where the mail bags would be found on the route, and then he left. I finished at noon, went home for lunch, and returned at 3:00 PM with the other carriers. I repeated this several more days, following the same routine Ed had laid out the previous summer.

Early the fourth day Mac cornered me. "Where were you between 12:00 and 3:00 PM the last few days?" I asked him what he meant when I indicated I had been delivering a route. He said, "I was tracking you and you finished at noon." So I told him that I went home for lunch and must have fallen asleep. He threatened, "If it happens again I'll have to fire you." He had been spying on me! And apparently he did so with the other carriers! "What Should I Do Now?" I had to slow down my pace and stretch out the time for three more hours!

I mentioned this to one of the carriers and he told me the whole story. "Mac had never carried a route and had no idea how much work it was. He thought he was going to impress upper management by being Mr. Tough Guy, and make big changes in our office. He tried to nitpick everything we did. He complained, found fault, bullied us, and told us to quit visiting and laughing with each other because it was unprofessional behavior which was against the rules. And he even drove around spying on us as we were carrying our routes, criticizing us for visiting with our customers! But we fought back! See that stack of mail on top of everyone's desk? That's the second-class stuff. We let it pile up, and Mac looks bad! We told him it takes us a lot of extra time constantly checking the rule book to be sure we were not breaking any rules which he will hold against us. He can't do a thing about that."

In another week, complaints from people who were not receiving their second-class mail reached Chicago, and officials from the main post office brought Ed back to replace Mac, who could not get the job done. In a few days all the stacked-up mail was delivered, and things were back to normal. Talking and laughter had returned. Mac was demoted back to the front office where he could do no more damage.

> **When good people run things, everyone is glad, but when the ruler is bad, Everyone groans. (Proverbs 29:2, The Message)**

Give me a leader with levity; that is, someone with a lighthearted touch who can find humor in everything that goes wrong or right. As they lead, they have fun, and they make sure the people they lead enjoy the ride, too. None of the people he or she leads feels threatened, but instead, they feel supported, defended, or assisted. One boss I had, Phil, was a daily demonstration of living his motto: *Because I have fun at what I do, nothing bad can happen where I'm in charge.* He proved that many times. One time in particular stands out.

Dale, a fellow engineer, came to Phil's office one day in a distraught condition. The conversation went something like this:

"Dale! What's wrong? You look sick!"
"I am. I just discovered a serious error in one of my calculations. The customer has already acted on it."

Dale had calculated how much concrete the customer should pour for containment walls to stand the pressure from an accidental broken pipe on the high-pressure nuclear reactor. His error would result in walls that were too thin.

Phil, our boss, told Dale, "Ease up, man. It's going to be okay! We can take care of that. Trust me. Check your calcs once more to be sure, and if they need more concrete, it will be okay! Trust me!"

Dale confirmed his error. Phil wrote a cheerful letter to the customer:

Dear Customer,

As you know, your power plant is being designed to be a showcase for the industry.

GE is always in the process of upgrading, checking, and improving our calculations. We find that in order to conservatively withstand pressures that could result from a pipe rupture, the containment wall thickness should be increased by one foot of reinforced concrete. Please include this in your construction.

The customer immediately wrote back:

Thank you. Please tell us where to add the concrete.

Dale responded to their query and turned out to be a hero, all because of a boss who had fun at what he did so that nothing bad could happen where he was in charge.

My second summer at the post office was good after Ed returned as boss of the mail carriers. Ed was more like Phil. Mac did not have the DNA for it. Ed was approachable, gentle, understanding. Mac was stiff, cold, and unfriendly. He seemed afraid of exposing his inability to respond in a meaningful, confident way--afraid he would embarrass himself, I think.

Kind words heal and help; cutting words wound and maim. (Proverbs 15:4)

Gracious speech is like clover honey—good taste to the soul, quick energy for the body. (Proverbs 16:24. The Message)

Phyllis and I were talking about a wedding the following summer. She stayed in Aurora to work while I planned to work on an engineering degree at Wisconsin. My goal was to become an engineer while being married to Phyllis, get hired by a company, write best-selling stories as a hobby, and to live happily ever after. I learned how easy it is for our direction to change when some of our goals are not quite realistic.

> We seldom can choose the person who will be our boss in a working environment. Some bosses are difficult and some are easy. Recall a boss you have either enjoyed or endured and describe what made it so. If he/she was difficult, how were you able to cope with that? If you had an especially good boss, what made him/her good from your viewpoint? If you become boss, what characteristics do you hope to possess to make you be seen as a good boss? What characteristics would you hope to avoid?

CHAPTER 19

COLLEGE TO UNIVERSITY—A BIG STRETCH!

After a year at Blackburn College I worked another summer at the post office. That paid for the fall semester at the University of Wisconsin, 100 miles from home, where five degrees in engineering were offered. I rented an apartment on Francis Street, up a hill from Lake Winona. Every morning I could hear the university crew team synchronized yelling from my third-floor room. Their rhythm was precise, but voice quality would not make opera.

Life at my apartment was a circus you could describe as *animal house* for guys. Every morning one of the *stranger* residents would waltz into the community bathroom asking permission to pop pimples and squeeze blackheads on the backs of the young men who were busy shaving at the sinks. Once someone lit and flushed a cherry bomb down a toilet, but it exploded too soon, blowing the commode apart. We had only three working stalls for 12 guys—a panic during rush hour.

My roommate Rex split the rent, which helped both of us. He wanted to quit smoking, but the agony was too much, and he could not shake the habit. He was the only smoker on our floor, and he often caused the hallway smoke alarm to go off, waking everyone up.

Rex was a wiry specimen who kept his beard perfectly trimmed. His passion was boxing. He claimed to have soaped the backs of several famous boxers after they won big fights. He smoked mostly in the hall, trying not to gas me out, but he wanted to quit so badly that he made a pact with the biggest guy on the floor: If that guy, who was built like a pro-wrestler, caught him smoking, he should either "beat the crap out of him or make him pay $10" (over a hundred bucks based on today's dollar). Rex nearly went out of his mind denying himself a cigarette the next day. Then he took ten dollars, paid the big guy, and lit up again.

One evening two guys in the next room lured the apartment cat, and spooned a combination of sardines and a diluted alcoholic beverage down its gullet. When I saw the cat later, it was attempting to navigate the hallway, staggering and bumping into walls. We did not see the cat for several days—it was probably nursing a hangover.

A friend told me I could get a job washing dishes at Alice's restaurant. She employed a few students and hired me to wash dishes early weekday mornings in exchange for breakfast and a late lunch (usually a ham salad sandwich). Alice was Norwegian and once a week she served *lutefisk* (fish soaked in lye—that's true! The kind you make soap with!) and *lefse* (like a tortilla, only made out of potatoes with a sprinkling of sugar—maybe). Some students, especially the Scandinavian ones, went crazy over the combination! The vile, rotten smell almost turned me inside out, and permeated her restaurant. I had no appetite on those days.

A requirement for first or second year male students was mandatory ROTC (Reserve Officer Training Corps). They fitted us with khaki-colored uniforms to wear on the day of ROTC class. We learned military science and how to shoot an M-1 rifle. I was the best marksman in my class of 50. It was a nice change of pace, getting to march in formation like one great machine with fifty other soldiers, even though we got barked at by the commanding officer. I learned of one recruit who showed up with a large circular hole in the back of his army-issued coat. His explanation: He laid it down and someone carelessly flicked a cigarette. The hole had smoldered before he found it and could douse the burn. He probably got a bill from the U.S. Army for one *see-through* dress coat.

With our wedding plans forming, Phyllis decided to work in a department store in Aurora while I was at Wisconsin. She decided to visit me one weekend and arrived by train on a Saturday morning in

October. There was no parlor for visitors in the animal house where I lived, so we spent time in the Student Union, and went to the afternoon football game at the stadium. It was during the time that *Alan The-Horse Ameche* was Wisconsin's star player. I don't remember if U. W. won or lost. Then we went to dinner and a movie. A young woman in my math class said Phyllis could spend the night at her apartment since her roommate would be out of town. After I picked Phyllis up Sunday morning, we got breakfast, found a church, visited with each other a while, went for lunch, and she boarded a train for home.

This was different. When I waved goodbye, got into my car, and drove away, I hurt inside for a long time. With her on the train, I could not control her departure, stop the train or run after it. It was almost like someone dying! The train pulls out and you have no control. My observation was that in saying goodbye, my reactions are opposite if I am on the train or left behind. I think it hurts more if I am left behind.

But the next weekend came soon. I continued to drive home weekends to see Phyllis, just like our visits the year before. Each time I returned to Wisconsin, it was harder to find a parking place. I was surprised and happy to learn that my high school friend, Don, lived in Madison. I called him and he said I could park my car at his home. A bus ran near it, which solved my parking problem.

When I told him about Phyllis, he offered to help me buy an engagement ring from Montgomery Ward's where he was a section manager. I used the rest of the money I had saved from my summer job as a down payment on the ring. I won't say that the diamond was small, but it came with a complimentary magnifying glass. Phyllis wore it proudly.

It was Christmastime and they welcomed me back to help carry residential mail routes for the post office. That finished paying for the ring. If Montgomery Ward's ever had to repossess the ring, they would have had to take Phyllis with it!

My grades at Wisconsin were average, and the reason was a compelling interest in writing fiction stories. I wanted to become an engineer, but I had a growing passion to become a story writer. I bought a three-inch thick book, *The Writing of Fiction*, which had lessons and exercises showing how to become a successful author. I spent most of my homework time in that book, dreaming of writing stories and getting paid for them. I wanted to follow that dream more than engineering. This was a time when I felt pulled in two different directions, and I had to let go of one or the other. I was asking myself, "What Should I Do Now?" I wish I had known God's promise,

Commit your works to the Lord, and your thoughts will be established. (Proverbs 16:3)

At the time, I did not know how to commit whatever I was doing to the Lord. Otherwise, my thoughts might have been clarified with His guidance. Eventually, He was able to prove the truth of that promise to me, but I put up a fight.. I was smart enough to know that even if I could write a novel in two weeks, the chances of getting it published and cashing in with enough money to set up housekeeping with a new wife were about zero. I had enough sense to realize that I should first take a path that led to a paying job. Engineering was the most logical path.

Before I left Wisconsin, I had one particular *adventure* at a bowling alley in Madison that had a dramatic effect on me—so dramatic it seemed worth documenting.

> Have you ever felt pulled in two different directions at the same time? One direction was driven by emotions and the other direction was driven by logic. How did you analyze which direction was best? You finally made a decision, but how did you made it.

CHAPTER 20

PINSETTER—LOWEST OF THE LOW

I was broke and desperate for five dollars to buy gas so I could drive from the University of Wisconsin to visit Phyllis in Aurora. Someone suggested I could sign up to set pins Friday evening at the student bowling alley. It paid $5.00 for two hours. I took his suggestion.

A big, muscular guy in the lane next to mine showed me how set the pins and keep from getting killed by high-speed bowling balls. They did not have automatic pinsetter machines. I had to gather all ten pins from the pit after one or two balls crashed and sent them flying. I dropped the pins into a triangular holder, pulled a lever to move them forward, set them down, and got out of the way. Immediately after that, the first bowling ball would come roaring down the lane and blast pins into the pit. After the second ball, I would have to do it again. There was no opportunity for distractions. One could easily be torpedoed by a high-speed ball and flying pins. The bowlers could not see the pinsetters who risked their lives, ignoring the fun and laughter at the far end of the lane.

I was glad no one could see me. I could not say for sure how the rest of the world looked at anyone who bore the title: *pinsetter*, but in the *pocket-book society* of the university campus, you would never find certain people setting pins. No football players, debate team members, fraternity brothers who drove convertibles with the top down, whose parents sent regular allowances so they could fully enjoy the college experience, crew team, scholarship people, honor roll people, student council movers and shakers, and those who made the dean's list last semester. None of them would be setting pins in a bowling alley.

On the college campus you could be a part-time waitress, draftsman, clerk, driver, or have another honorable part-time job. But pin-setting? That was a job for *losers*. This was embarrassing—an admission that I was broke and unsuccessful. A beggar! A leech! A drag on society! Scum! It was a job no one else wanted. But I kept reminding myself that I was not a *loser* and my short identification with campus *losers* would be over in two hours. Then I could forget it forever as I was in my 1940 Chevy (not a hot convertible) driving to see the special young woman who had become so much a part of my life.

The big guy setting pins in the next lane was hefty, twice my size, strong as an ox with extra pounds he really did not need. Consequently, he was slow in replacing the pins. When my pins were set and I was safely perched, I noticed that a trio was bowling in his lane, consisting of two college girls and one boy, who was a show-off wearing a polo shirt monogrammed with the Greek name of his fraternity. I would best describe his mannerisms as *cute*. The girls giggled, and this prompted him to act cuter. Since the hefty pinsetter was slow, the *cute* guy made snide remarks, loud enough for the pinsetter to hear. "I wonder if he's on lunch break." The girls giggled. Then after setting up my pins again, I heard the *cute* guy refer once more to their pinsetter, "I wonder if he's reading a comic book and can't be disturbed?" More giggling from the girls. Finally, "I wonder if he's resting up for his garbage collection job in the morning." That did it!

The triangular holder that delivered ten pins to the lane had just risen up, leaving the pins ready for the next bowling ball in the "cute" guy's lane, but it never came. Suddenly two bulging, muscular arms pushed through the ten pins, knocking them over, half to the left and half to the right as the hefty pinsetter climbed out of the pit onto the lane on his hands and knees, stood up, at least six feet tall, and started walking briskly toward the giggling girls and the "cute" guy, who stood frozen, holding a bowling ball. As the pinsetter approached them, the girls stopped giggling. There were no snide remarks—just three wide open mouths and wide eyes. The ball fell out of the guy's hands crashing on the lane as he turned and fled, not stopping to take off the bowling shoes and collect his own. I imagined that he hurried for refuge back to a fraternity house where he would find protection and be able to boast about some "low life that was turtle-slow setting pins at the bowling alley." Of course he would leave out the part where he dirtied his underwear, and left two girls to find their own transportation home. The pinsetter said something to the girls like, "If you two want to continue the game, I'll set it up." Then he returned to the pit next to me.

Maybe this exposes some weird part of my personality, but because of that incident, I confess that I was suddenly proud to be identified with the lowest of the low! I am like them! I am like that hefty pinsetter! We have feelings, too. We have aspirations. Hopes. Dreams. Pride. When someone disparages us, it hurts. When the ones who laugh and belittle us are challenged with no place to hide, it shows that underneath their bold, tough talk, they are really cowardly wimps. They are powerless in a real encounter. Who they pretend to be is to impress others until they are exposed to show who they really are. I suddenly felt a kinship with my hefty pinsetter neighbor. For that evening, I was proud to be identified with him—I was a proud member of the *lower than low pinsetters*!

There is a Bible verse that says,

> ***the Lord does not see as man sees; for man looks at the outward appearance, but the Lord looks at the heart. (I Samuel 16:7 b)***

That verse suggests a good perspective to live by whether you are a religious person or not. Whatever our social status, what kind of car we drive, what job we work, what degree of education we have, or how expensive a house we own—underneath all those trimmings we are people with feelings, hopes, dreams, the capacity to give and receive love, to care, and to make a difference in each other's lives. *Looking on the heart* can make us more than we could ever make of ourselves.

As a plus, now I had gas money for the drive to Aurora.

> Is it hard for you to feel comfortable with people from another country, a different culture, another race, economic or educational status, or from the other side of the tracks, setting pins in the bowling lane next to you? Would you say that your feelings are normal or the symptoms of a problem? If you are someone who looks to the Bible for guidance, how would you view your feelings in light of Genesis 1:27 which states, *So God created man in His own image; in the image of God He created man;..*

CHAPTER 21

THE WINDY CITY

After one semester at the University of Wisconsin, and not getting the best grades because I spent too much time trying to write my first novel, I changed plans. Phyllis would be willing to work and put me through school at the University of Colorado so I could get my engineering degree out of the way. To keep in classroom practice during the spring semester, I moved to Chicago, *The Windy City*, where I attended night school at the Illinois Institute of Technology (IIT). The main reason was to be closer to Phyllis in Aurora, one hour away instead of several from Wisconsin, and to take a reduced course load. Since the weekend drive to Aurora was shorter, Phyllis and I could begin wedding plans. I rented a tiny room at the YMCA where homework kept me too busy to notice how cramped it was.

My room was closet-sized with a bed, clothes cabinet, walking space between the bed and cabinet, one chair at the foot, and a window just beyond the chair. The only door at the head of the bed opened into the hall with a community bathroom 20 yards away. Cozy.

I hung my suit in the cabinet and draped my white shirt over the chair in front of the window that was opened one inch for fresh air. That was a mistake because I found a dark gray stripe across my shirt in the morning from the *windy city's soot*! Each night I sat with my legs up on the bed leaning against a pillow propped against the wall with a single light bulb dangling overhead, doing homework on a clipboard. There was no phone, TV or other distraction except the elevator "ding" in the hallway. Also absent were yelling and loud voices like at Blackburn and Wisconsin, and I missed that—a little.

My two courses were *Differential Equations* and *Beginning Psychology*. The math professor came to class the evening after Einstein died, announcing that one of us would have to take his place (all chuckled). Besides doing math homework with a backache (the pillow did not give enough support), the Einstein announcement was the high point of the class. However, the psychology class had practical value. I could identify negative personalities. Over the years, I think the negative personality types conspired to make life miserable for me in one way or another. Some of those with "personality disorders" occupied teacher and management positions over me, giving an opportunity for me to privately analyze them while I tried to determine the best way to respond to their narcissistic, self-promoting directions. I did eventually learn how to find humor in the discomfort some of them caused.

I needed a daytime job and was hired immediately to sell shoes at the Chicago Faire Store in the children's department. I thought I had graduated from selling shoes, but maybe having little kids for customers would be fun—if their mothers didn't interfere too much! Mr. Mandell was manager for both the children's and adult shoes. He was heavy, bald with a few white temple hairs, double chins, and a scowl that would stop a stampede! The clerks gave him a lot of space as he waddled around both departments without a word.

We sold shoes on 8% commission and 53.00 dollars a week guaranteed, but if we didn't sell enough to make 53.00 in commissions, we went in the hole. Some clerks would never catch up. Your sales depended on how fast you could find shoes in the stacks and how many customers you could corral at one time. It was my first *dog-eat-dog* competition. A veteran clerk agreed that I could come in for no pay on my day off and learn the stacks better. Mr. Mandell saw me browsing and growled the first words he ever spoke to me: "What the hell are you doing here? It's your day off!" I explained I wanted to learn the shoe locations on my own time. "Get the hell out of here," he roared, "And don't come back 'til you're supposed to be here!" The other clerks stood like statues while the sound of his voice echoed away. None of them made eye contact with me. "What should I do now?" I picked up my jacket and headed to the elevator. The "Ruler-Potentate of All" had spoken. There could be no resistance.

> *You who are servants, be good servants to your masters—not just to good masters, but also to bad ones. What counts is that you put up with it for God's sake when you're treated badly for no good reason. There's no particular virtue in accepting punishment that you well deserve. But if you're treated badly for good behavior and continue in spite of it to be a good servant, that is what counts with God. This is the kind of life you've been invited into, the kind of life Christ lived. He suffered everything that came His way so you would know that it could be done, and also know how to do it step-by-step.* **(I Peter 2:18-20, The Message)**

I learned one lesson from the Mandell episode: Whenever you want to do *anything* that departs from the normal processes or procedures, check first with the *big boss*, even if it is good for all concerned and has *no downsides* that you can see. He needs to know that you know he is in control. If he says, "Don't bother me with such trifles, just do them!", then that is different. But give him the chance to give you the go-ahead with the trifles.

Mr. Mandell was one more grumpy boss I had encountered. That was my biased point of view. Maybe others saw him as a kind gentleman--a jolly old Santa Claus. I did feel sorry for the man. He always was alone, without friends. Other than delivering critical remarks, he never talked to anyone or socialized with other employees—at the water cooler, in the lunch room, or anywhere else. (I couldn't vouch for the men's room. I suppose perpetual constipation can make you mean and ugly.) Anytime he spoke, it was negative, cutting, threatening. He seemed to enjoy being feared. Sad. One thing that helped—I knew that God had something better for my future; I had survived previous grumpy bosses; this job was not going to last forever; and I probably needed this old grouch to toughen me up for worse experiences with more disagreeable bosses.

There was one more shoe department episode. It exposed a *degenerate* change that I think can ruin some people when they are promoted or honored. Mr. Grey was one of the friendly shoe clerks in the children's department under Mr. Mandell. He gave me helpful hints on how to work with little customers—kids, and especially the unruly ones who came for new shoes. It was decided that the *children's shoes* department was big enough to be separated from the adult shoe department, and Mr. Grey would be the manager. The other clerks were happy to be out from under Mr. Mandell's thumb and have a manager they knew and liked.

But something happened to Mr. Grey overnight. He was no longer the friendly, warm, *one-of-us* people he used to be. Suddenly he grew cold. He was "Mr. Tough Manager" who claimed that there was *a new captain at the helm.* The children's department would function differently under his direction. It was going to become a *showcase, top sales department* in the Faire Store. High sales, shipshape, efficient, high ratings by customers, and every positive adjective you can find in the dictionary. Mr. Grey would be unstoppable. His tone was tyrannical. He turned from being a coach, mentor, and friend to an all-business dictator. Rude. Impersonal. Untouchable. Critical. If a potential customer left the floor without purchasing, he wanted a full report on why. He insisted on using increased pressure to sell.

The other clerks no longer enjoyed their work. Once I was putting shoes back in the stacks where Mr. Grey was taking inventory. He asked, "Fred, do I make you feel inferior?" I answered, "No." That probably wasn't the answer he was looking for because he began to criticize everything I did with a vengeance! He grew angry and found fault with how I approached, talked with, even laughed with customers—everything I did was wrong! Many times I wondered, "What Should I Do Now?"

Mr. Grey bullied me at every opportunity. If there was no opportunity, he went out of his way to invent one. Taking Psychology 101 at night school didn't qualify me to make a professional diagnosis, but I could see that his promotion had destroyed him. It made him lose his bearings. The clerks who used to be his friends were now *objects* to help him gain importance. He didn't smile any more. We were *stepping stones* or *obstacles* that helped or hindered his progress. His self-view was different. The world revolved around him! The psycho-term is "narcissism" "The most important person is me!" I discovered that the Bible speaks against this self-view:

> *For I say, through the grace given to me, to everyone who is among you, not to think of himself more highly than he ought to think, but to think soberly, as God has dealt to each one a measure of faith. (Romans, 12:3)*
>
> *Let nothing be done through selfish ambition or conceit, but in lowliness of mind let each esteem other better than himself. (Philippians, 2:3)*
>
> *When the righteous are in authority, the people rejoice; but when a wicked man rules, the people groan. (Proverbs, 29:2)*
>
> *Let another man praise you, and not your own mouth; a stranger, and not your own lips. (Proverbs, 27:2)*

When people think of themselves as more important than everyone else, they lose friends and joy in whatever they are doing. If they are unhappy, the whole world is dismal and their satisfaction comes from making others unhappy, too. They cannot identify someone to share life with on either a superficial or deeper level. They can't name anyone who feels the same way they do. They are not close enough to anyone who will listen when they want to share their feelings. They have no one who really cares about how they feel. Someone once said, "It's lonely at the top." I suppose it is if you climb there by yourself, stepping on your friends like Mr. Grey was doing.

It was two more weeks and the semester at IIT was over. When I left my job, Mr. Grey offered no kind parting words, but the clerks expressed their good wishes. I gathered all my belongings from the YMCA in a single shopping bag and left (there were no embroidered linens to include as souvenirs like you might find at the *Ritz*). Phyllis and I were again in Aurora, working at jobs and planning a fall wedding. After the ceremony we would move to Boulder, Colorado. Phyllis would work while I studied at the university.

Years have passed since my painful days working for two grumpy, maladjusted Faire Store bosses. Even though they both seemed designed to make life miserable for their workers, they gave me something of value:

They gave me negative role models I would never want to imitate.

I also learned that I could survive in a closet-sized apartment.

> If you have worked at different jobs, there is no way you could avoid having at least one boss with a personality defect that made him or her difficult to work for. Imagine that your fellow employees expressed amazement that in spite of the boss, you enjoyed your work; you were always upbeat and cheerful; and you never spoke an unkind word about anyone including the boss. How were you able to react in this way?

FACING THE CHALLENGES

CHAPTER 22

WEDDING BELLS

A week before our wedding, I sat on Phyllis's back steps showing her dad my savings book. I wanted to put his mind at ease that I could take care of his daughter forever and still attend school, since she would find a job to pay for incidentals like food and rent. He smiled, puffing on a cigar, and said knowingly, "That's nice."

It was a high speed week for everyone attending to the details. Phyllis and I joked about eloping, just to reduce the chaos. I learned that staying out of sight was my safest strategy, since there was nothing I could do when it came to making logical suggestions as Phyllis's mom and several women of her church were deciding on final plans for the event. To interfere could be life-threatening—to me! They ultimately crafted the absolute best setting, overflowing with their love and best wishes without my help.

The ceremony was like a scaled-down Broadway production. My best man, a devout Catholic friend I had met at Blackburn, had to get a special dispensation from his priest to participate in a Baptist church wedding without being consumed by the flames of God's wrath! But he said that doing it for a friend was worth the sacrifice of having to go to confession regularly for three months, doing a string of Hail Mary's, and possibly providing a Cuban cigar, a bottle of Scotch, and a piece of wedding cake for the priest. All he did was hand me the ring.

The wedding was over in a flash and we were off to Boulder, Colorado. We moved into a low rent back-alley apartment that used to be a porch attached to a bedroom wall, but was now open to the land-lady's two-story house. Mrs. Stuart lived in the front part and had two tenants upstairs. She was hard of hearing. We had little privacy since we had to share a bathroom with her, which separated our apartment from hers with hanging blue curtains instead of doors. She also had cockroaches which we held at bay with lethal blue powder around the perimeter of each room and all window sills.

At night we sometimes heard "clicking" from her apartment. Once, we tiptoed with a flashlight through the bathroom and its two curtains directly into her kitchen to see what was making the sounds. We saw uncovered pieces of venison on her kitchen table with cockroaches swarming on them. "Click!" Another cockroach appeared on the table out of nowhere! Cockroaches on the ceiling were dropping onto the table. We shuddered and went back to our own safe space, putting a refresher layer of blue powder across the doorway. We didn't know how to tell Mrs. Stuart what we saw without admitting we were nosing around. Then we decided to tell her we heard a strange sound and when we checked for burglars, we saw the cockroaches. I think that stopped her from leaving out uncovered food.

One day Phyllis said I needed a haircut so I was at the mercy of Ed in a barber's chair. It was the only barber shop in a strip mall across from the university campus. Ed's magnetic personality made me feel like we were life-long friends. While he clipped my hair, he grilled me like a friendly trial lawyer. He put on the finishing touches and insisted that now I looked more like a movie star than a shaggy dog. He still kept talking after I had paid and started toward the door. But Ed wasn't through with me.

He walked me out to the sidewalk, blabbering nonstop. I managed to get a few words in when he took a breath. His patter transitioned to *ballroom dancing*. Phyllis and I had gone to high-school dances. In fact, that's how we met—it was a *Sadie-Hawkins* event where the girls asked the guys to escort them. All I knew was the square-step my mother taught me, but I knew enough to keep me from stepping on Phyllis's toes, which might have ended our beginning interest in each other. Ed dripped with enthusiasm as he described the magical world of dancing and how it was the key to a *blossoming social life*. He persuaded me that dancing would be a valuable investment. My reaction was a "This is it!" moment that drove me to a decision. Ballroom dancing was something Phyllis and I had to do! How fortunate that destiny put me in touch with Ed!

The compulsion was verified. We were standing on the sidewalk in front of the barber shop—next to the doorway of an Arthur Murray Dance Studio! Fate? Fortune? It seemed too much of a coincidence to be a coincidence! But there was more. Ed was one of the dance instructors, teaming up with a young couple who ran the studio. A ten-lesson package cost $100. That was the amount of cash gifts we had received at our wedding! Did I need more evidence that this had to be part of our life plan, *written in the stars*?

When I told Phyllis, her reaction was similar to mine. Besides, the University sponsored several dances during the year so we could apply our training. We signed up and paid cash.

The couple who ran the studio demonstrated a dance step each week to music from a cheap 78 rpm phonograph. After each demo, the woman worked with the men, and her husband with the women. Ed assisted with some of us who were confused by the terms "left" and "right" every time we reversed direction.

Then we practiced with our spouses while the phonograph played over and over until the hour of agony (for me) ended. Each week was a different step: Latin and Rhythm, Rumba, Mambo, Cha-Cha, Swing, Hop, Waltz, Foxtrot, Tango, Country, Polka, or Two-step. There was no review of the previous week's step! I think each step was supposed to be branded on our brain forever! We graduated with a handshake, a typewritten "Arthur Murray Certificate of Completion," and $100 poorer.

With our new ability, I had to ask, "What Should We Do Now?" The *social value test* would come at the *homecoming dance*. We dressed up in the only party threads we owned, which smelled like mothballs.

Hoping that the music might coax out the dance steps buried inside, we entered the dimly-lit university ballroom. Everything after that is a blurred series of memory flashes, so the following description is a disorganized montage.

Our first impression was the surprising party atmosphere. We were expecting a somber mood because the Colorado Golden Buffaloes had lost the homecoming football game that afternoon. When our eyes adjusted to the dim light, we stepped along the sidelines trying not to disrupt the gawkers, who were watching dancers, looking for friends, or scanning the large room for a restroom sign. We searched in vain for a familiar face. No one was there from the dance class, my engineering classes, Phyllis's friends from the records office, and none of my professors. We spied two chairs in a *safety zone* and grabbed them. The band across the room was dedicated to drown out conversation, so we couldn't talk and be heard above the noise.

When you have known someone long enough, you can communicate by your own sign language. You also can make faces—roll your eyes, shake your head, smile, and frown. That's what we did as we studied couples wobbling on the dance floor. It was more fun than dancing! Some couples passed by in a *stiff-arm* pose, arms extended, rigid elbows, and distance enough to ride a bicycle between them. Maybe one of them needed breath mints. Several couples were *glued together* with feet welded to the floor. Their ankles were hinges as their upper bodies swayed rhythmically back-and-forth, east-west-north-and-south. It was their imitation of a sunflower bending in the breeze.

I cannot forget one couple that alarmed me. The brute held the girl captive in a death grip against him. It looked like she was trying to call for help but could not inhale! Furthermore, if she had arrived with normal proportions, she would go home flat-chested. The dance floor was one moving sideshow! We had good seats for the price of admission!

They blew a trumpet and cleared the floor as a formally-dressed couple, not part of the *herd*, began a graceful number, gliding from one end of the room to the other. They embraced, whirled, held hands, spun, twirled, twisted. He lifted her over his head as she soared like a butterfly; she flew into his arms as he scooped her high into a flutter, synchronized with enchanting, recorded music. (The band was on a break, thank goodness!) The elegant couple ended their performance with a bow to a standing ovation. (Standing because there weren't that many chairs and we had claimed two of them!)

After that, couples trickled onto the dance floor like cattle crowding into a corral. We edged our way to the door and drove home. For the first time that evening we could talk to each other without being shut down by a loud dance band. We couldn't help short bursts of laughter, recounting the mutilated dance steps we saw. The artistic couple was a treat that made the evening a *winner*. It did not matter if there was the crowd of several hundred pushing, shoving couples trying to stay vertical on a hardwood floor—or just the two of us. We had fun!

Ed may be right that ballroom dancing is the key to a *blossoming social life* for some, but not for us. I discovered that ballroom dancing is a lot like college football—which can be a four- year scholarship to a star high-school football player; but to most, it is a sporting event to be enjoyed by faithful fans.

We enjoyed being spectators at the dance, but we would not have enjoyed being *players*. Choosing to take dance lessons as the key to a blossoming social life was a bad choice because it resulted in an unnecessary loss of time and money. The dance lessons had been useless based on their advertised value. They did not launch our social life. Our social life thrived from other sources like book clubs, yard parties, home Bible studies, hobby clubs, travel clubs, going to lectures, out to dinner, movies, and even a rodeo with friends.

Although the dance lessons were a loss, the experience of making a bad choice exposed one of my weaknesses that had to be fixed to avoid a *next time*. I needed something to help me guard against another bad choice where I might be suckered into buying something or making a commitment that would be another bad choice—like a "can't lose" financial investment, a new, unaffordable vehicle, a time-share membership, a special discount insurance policy, a monthly health supplement that Big Pharma and the medical profession do not want you to know about—and the "must have" list is never-ending. I needed a *life principle* that had built-in protection from myself.

Two Proverbs from Solomon give the *insurance plan* I was looking for:

The simple believes every word, but the prudent considers well his steps. *(Proverbs 14:15)*

Commit your works to the Lord, and your thoughts will be established. *(Proverbs 16:3)*

"To consider" means to think carefully about a matter, especially in *making a decision*. That implies drawing mental pictures of the outcome of a decision, showing the near- and long-term results of the steps involved. Reasoning where the steps lead, it should become clear if that is realistically what we expect, or if our emotions have camouflaged reality.

"To commit" what we do to the Lord is to release it and offer it to Him for His purpose. If we can trustingly do this, and not protectively hang on to our works, according to Solomon, our thoughts should grow in line with the Lord's will for making right choices.

> Sadly, you know what it's like when someone has sold you a "must have" device, investment, or process. His or her sales pitch was credible, sincere, supported by data and trials, and you felt no pressure. It turned out he was a "B-Ser" selling "BS." and you took the bait. How can you protect yourself in the future?

CHAPTER 23

LOOK BEFORE YOU LEAP

I got decent grades the first semester at the University of Colorado, which ended in January, and we had spent our savings on tuition, books, and a toaster. Out-of-state tuition would be due in a few weeks and I couldn't write a check for it, even with Phyllis's income. But I still had this growing passion to be a fiction writer, so we decided I should drop out for one or two semesters, get a daytime job and write in the evenings and on weekends. My passion for engineering was lower than pumping septic tanks, compared to my passion for writing fiction.

I found a job as an engineering assistant with Micro-Switch in Denver. The day before I was to start work, Mrs. Stewart came to the bathroom curtain calling, "Long distance for Fred!" It was Micro-Switch. Since I had not been in military service, I would be fair game for the draft. The company didn't want to train me and then lose me to the draft. The job vanished. "Thanks anyway," I said, looking out the window at falling snow. "What's wrong?" Phyllis asked through her pin curlers. I explained, saying that it looked like God was holding us hostage, keeping me in school while He sent us to the poor house. I thought God didn't care about our meager situation. It was one of many times I had to ask, "What Should I Do Now?"

The spring semester had just begun so I registered late, hoping somehow to arrange a late tuition payment. My request was met with a surprise! Because Phyllis worked for the university, the cashier told me I was eligible for in-state tuition, which was much less than out-of-state! Maybe God actually did care after all!

The financial weight of tuition was lifted, and I began to enjoy engineering. The world would have to wait for my spellbinding novels.

When a year had passed, one professor asked me to be his grader, which meant I would grade the homework and tests turned in by his students. That was a challenge, especially when it came to the tests, since I had to work them first before I could grade them. Even though I had taken his course, I struggled with some of the problems, but learned a lot.

A young couple we knew from high school moved to Boulder with their daughter. The dad was hired as chief draftsman at a new company called *Control Cells*, a division of *Ball Brothers Research*. He made archive drawings for the manufacture of a new invention and hired me as a part-time assistant, which supplemented Phyllis's income. The trucking industry at that time knew how to avoid weighing stations and they got away with overloads on the highways. Consequently, the highway patrol failed to collect huge fines. Control Cells designed portable scales for the highway patrol to carry in the trunks of their patrol cars so they could stop and weigh trucks and vans anywhere on any highway—and usually assess overload fines.

I was a student in need of a design project, so I played defense for the truckers. I invented a way for Control Cells to use their portable scales to also help the truckers avoid the overload fines. It used blinking lights to help load a truck so that all axles carried legal shares of the total load. One of my professors urged me to patent the device, but that was too expensive. Instead, the professor and several students signed each page of a document describing it.

I sealed it in an envelope and mailed it to myself to prove it was my idea in case someone else claimed it. Getting a patent was extremely important if an inventor wanted to protect his or her idea. For me, getting a decent grade in a class was all that mattered.

The invention won second place in a contest sponsored by The American Society of Mechanical Engineers. The sealed envelope is still in a box somewhere, unopened many years later. I thought at one time if I ever become famous, the envelope and its contents might have historical value in a local museum. (Is that vain? Otherwise, the individual pages will be useful for the bottom of the cage of some lucky bird.)

I was beginning to see that the way things were shaping up in our life together could not be coincidences any more. The only explanation that made sense to me was that God was looking out for us: Closing the door by keeping me in school, lowering the tuition payment, giving me part-time jobs to help our finances—and at the time, I was not strong enough spiritually to even pray about those things. He just made things happen in spite of me.

Control Cells was moving ahead with my idea. Even if I got a job offer more in line with my interests (I didn't want to be a draftsman forever), CC could make my invention one of their sales products and pay me a royalty on all profits. Things were looking pretty good for us. Nothing could possibly go wrong—or could it? Maybe I would decide prayer could help.

Commit your works to the Lord, and your thoughts will be established. (Proverbs 16:3)

> Things are going good. No threats that you can see. Everything is on course in your life. All seems to be well. Why do you think some people worry more at times like that? Are you one of them? Do you proceed with caution? Do you worry that something is bound to go wrong? If so, is this a psychological or spiritual problem that you can fix?

CHAPTER 24

SHIPWRECKED SECURITY

I was busy at my drafting table one afternoon where I had a part-time job with *Ball Brothers Research*. The boss's secretary surprised me with an envelope containing a short note: *Mr. Safford would like the pleasure of meeting with you at 3:00 PM today in his office.*

My drafting job had been an unexpected surprise. Paul, a high school friend, had moved to Boulder. He took every mechanical drawing class offered in high school and now was hired as manager of the drafting department at *Control Cells*. He needed a part-time assistant and since I had drawing pencils, erasers, and a tee-square, he hired me. Phyllis and I were getting by on her salary from the university records office while I took classes, but with this job, we could afford a nicer apartment. We moved to a larger, clean upstairs apartment, a step up from our back-alley enclosed porch which we had shared with cockroaches.

Paul was a fine manager in our two-person drafting department. He was relaxed and fun-loving with a good sense of humor. Phyllis and I became close friends with his wife and young daughter. Paul was content with *who he was,* and he had no aspiration for a college degree. He celebrated the fact that I was nearing graduation, unlike Homer, the labor foreman I had worked for several years earlier. Comparing Paul and Homer I learned that:

> *If a person is happy with who they are, they are happy with who other people are.*

That was Paul. He liked what he did and was good at it. He appreciated and supported what others did. I also learned that

> *If a person is unhappy with who they are, they are unhappy with who other people are.*

That was Homer, and he showed his disdain for me by making fun of my going to college. His remarks did not hide his feelings. For example: "Don't give Mr. College Man anything to do—he'll screw it up!" Occasionally, I thought that no matter who my future managers would be after graduation, I probably would never have a manager quite as enjoyable as Paul.

But now it was time for the three o'clock meeting. Mr. Safford was not only the big boss, but also the founder of *Control Cells,* the branch company I was working for part-time. He, too, was friendly, soft-spoken and cheerful. The meeting could only be something good. His company involved portable scale systems for weighing large semi-trucks anywhere on the highway, not only at weight stations. Colorado truckers habitually overloaded their trucks and got away with it. The highway patrol welcomed the idea of stopping a truck, weighing all axles, and fining the trucking company if a truck was overloaded. The device was still in design and testing stages, and my job was to make manufacturing drawings.

That was not the best part. I had suggested another possible market—for the trucking companies (described in Chapter 23). It was "playing both ends against the middle," because it would help the truckers avoid being overloaded! I had an invention to go with my idea: a string of lights to be hung up in an empty truck from front to back with each truck axle on a set of the scales. As the truck was being loaded, the lights would turn on telling the loaders to keep loading back toward the rear. When the last light went on, the truck would have its load distributed with the legal maximum payload. *Control Cells* liked that ideas, and so did trucking companies. I presented the concept at a student contest of the American Society of Mechanical Engineers and it won

Second Place! I imagined that Mr. Safford wanted to talk about getting a patent on the "Trailer Load Planner."

I knocked on the boss's door as my heart was beating with high expectation. The chief engineer, Willis, opened the door and welcomed me. The chief test engineer, Dick, stood up to greet me. Mr. Safford stood up for a moment, but remained behind his desk. He motioned for me to take the only empty chair opposite him. He began by expressing appreciation for my efforts in the Company, especially since I was only a part-time employee. So far, so good!

Then he lowered his tone. "When we started this venture two years ago we had the highest hopes. We did our best to cover all the bases. Since our device depends on accurate measurements, it had to be scrutinized…." He began to name agencies like the Bureau of Weights and Measures, the Bureau of Commerce, and certain laboratories. He rambled on, but I could tell that wherever he was going—it wasn't going to be pretty. He ended by saying, "We have to dissolve the company because there is no way our design can be brought up to commercial standards. Everyone will get a severance package. You will get two week's pay." It was like the bright summer sun suddenly fell out of the sky into the ocean, leaving darkness.

Time froze for a moment. No one in the office moved or said anything, but my thoughts whirled. My job was essential, I thought. We needed both Phyllis's and my paychecks to pay the rent on our better apartment and manage all our other expenses! We would be back with the cockroaches! We couldn't save money for graduation and travel to somewhere when I got a job offer. I took a deep breath and felt an unstoppable panic radiating from the middle of my chest to every extremity! "Oh, no!" were the only words that came out! Then I got up and paced back and forth holding my head. Still, no one offered a word. I don't remember anything more of that meeting. I went to the drafting room to get my jacket, pencils, and other things and drove home to tell Phyllis.

On the drive home I was thinking, "An hour ago I was content, secure, and happy because everything was *stacked* in our favor. Everything was painless and comfortable. The future was filled with exciting prospects. Now it was shipwrecked! Happiness, joy, comfort, security—was blown away in a moment! " I groaned as I parked in front of our apartment. I saw myself as the victim under attack without weapons powerful enough to fight back. That frame of mind leads to giving up, unless you can think of a unique solution to fight back, or you can call on a resource bigger and stronger than you are to fight your battle. I was not aware of the biblical truth written in the Psalms by David:

Call upon Me in the day of trouble; I will deliver you, and you shall glorify Me. (Psalm 50:15)

or with the comfort offered by his wise son, Solomon:

The name of the Lord is a strong tower; The righteous run to it and are safe. (Proverbs 18:10)

If had only sensed that God was close to me and cared what was happening at the time, I would have called on Him and rushed to Him, explained my situation as I saw it, asked Him to help me see it through His eyes, and to give me wisdom to know what I should do. Then I would have known the peace that He gives when the proverbial roof falls in. But I didn't know His consoling capacity then, so I had to look to myself to fight the battle, asking. "What Should I Do Now?"

Ideas kept running through my mind before Phyllis came home from her job. Where could I find another part-time job? Would I have to wait tables and work for tips? Deliver pizzas? Pump gas at a mini-market? I asked for yesterday's newspaper from the family in the downstairs apartment. When I searched the want-ads the name "Beech Aircraft" kept popping up. It was a local company, which listed a number of job openings. Hope began to rise. More want ads for technical people at Beech! I started composing a resume'.

I heard Phyllis's footsteps on the stairs and greeted her. "Let's talk," I said. Her smile disappeared, but I was overflowing with optimism. I described what Mr. Safford had said, but before she could react, I told her of my plan to apply for a job at Beech. When I paused and she finally did get a chance to speak, she said, "You know, we don't have to worry about this." I was a bit jolted when she said that—not by her words, but it was as if she already knew what was going to happen, and it was good. Between that evening and the next morning my outlook was bubbling with expectation. Even if I didn't get a job right away I wouldn't panic again! But Phyllis had said, almost prophetically, "We don't have to worry about this!" The next day I was interviewed by the chief engineer at Beech Aircraft and he hired me as a part-time engineer's assistant to work whatever hours fit with my classes!

Hope deferred makes the heart sick, but when the desire comes, it is a tree of life. (Proverbs 13:12)

> Think of a time when you could hardly wait for something. Your expectations were at their highest—and the whole thing "crumbled." Did you find an answer to, "What Should I Do Now?" If you are still looking for an answer, sometimes when you tell someone else what happened, the answer becomes clear. Why not try it?

CHAPTER 25

DRAFTSMAN TO ENGINEERING ASSISTANT (?)

I started at Beech Aircraft as an engineering assistant (*doormat* would have been a better description) for Sam W. at a garage where Dewars were stored before shipment to military bases. A Dewar, I learned, is a small-size tank truck for transporting liquefied gas. My job was to verify external measurements of the vehicles—height, length, diameters, and to record bolt sizes in a notebook.

This was obviously a *make-work* job—a useless exercise! These vehicles wouldn't be in this garage ready for shipment unless they had undergone final approval! I asked Sam why this duplicate effort was required. "Just do it. That's the job description," he snorted. From that time, he nitpicked everything I did. I could tell that he did not like to be challenged. It made him uncomfortable. Why? Simply this: *Sam was one of those people who was unhappy with who he was, and therefore, he could not be happy with others.*

I learned that Sam had started college but had dropped out to work for Beech. He seemed smart and fit for a job above his present position. Maybe he regretted dropping out of school. I was nearing graduation and Sam's career was sitting in an office drinking coffee, playing cards with another manager, emerging every hour to check on me, the only employee under his authority. He always found fault with whatever I was doing. I was too slow or not paying attention to color codes, or I was measuring Row A before Row B when I should alternate one from A then one from B, as if it made any difference. He enjoyed cutting me down. I came close to losing it and telling him I thought the only way he could bolster his own importance was to diminish someone else—but I painfully held it in. Years later I found a couple of biblical truths that would have soothed my throbbing state of mind:

It is honorable for a man to stop striving, since any fool can start a quarrel. (Proverbs 20:3) Do not say, "I will recompense evil"; Wait for the Lord, and He will save you. (Proverbs 20:22)

Beloved, do not avenge yourselves, but rather give place to wrath; for it is written, "Vengeance is Mine, I will repay," says the Lord. (Romans 12:19)

I did the right thing without knowing it by keeping my mouth shut, but nailing Sam with choice words that would injure him would be satisfying, I thought. At least the biblical truths imply that the Lord will even the score somehow in His own way, and I should accept that like an umpire's call even though I might have called it otherwise. The umpire calls it a "strike," and I know it was a "ball." I am not supposed to attack the umpire with the bat, although I wish I could, at times.

If I had ever held the image that God was like a rich uncle who would do anything to make us happy, my image was crumbling. There are verses showing that the Lord looks at our scorched feelings differently than we do. Although we are the ones who may be hurting, it is written (and I still don't particularly like it),

You who are servants, be good servants to your masters—not just to good masters, but also to bad ones. What counts is that you put up with it for God's sake when you're treated badly for no good reason. There's no particular virtue in accepting punishment that you well deserve. But if you're treated badly for good behavior and continue in spite of it to be a good servant, that is what counts with God. This is the kind of life you've been invited into, the kind of life Christ lived. He suffered everything that came His way so you would know that it could be done, and also know how to do it step by step. (I Peter 2: 18-21; The Message)

I decided that working for Sam was a road to nowhere, so I politely listened, gritted my teeth, and went about the tasks my own way.

After enduring two weeks of Sam, I found a message in my time card slot: "Ralph needs you in the drafting department." I thought, "Hooray! Rescued from futility!" Ralph was an older gentleman in charge of 30 draftsmen, and he needed someone to occupy the drawing board next to his. I never had a tearful goodbye with Sam, and I don't know (nor do I care) if he grieved over losing his one subordinate. Ralph gave me trivial machine parts to draw 3-D views for manufacturing.

Something in Ralph's department didn't seem right. The other draftsmen sat at their tables reading magazines or books. None of them were drawing! When I introduced myself and asked several of them what they were working on, they said, "Nothing! Nothing at all!" They were ready to work if Beech got a government contract they were bidding on. These men were needed to advertise a fully staffed company at all levels, both technical and administrative. In truth, the idle draftsmen were salaried window-dressing and I was too!

These draftsmen were in a holding period of idleness, not by their choice, or by laziness on their part. Choosing inactivity for comfort or convenience is known to cause deterioration:

Because of laziness the building decays, and through idleness of hands the house leaks. (Ecclesiastes 10:10)

I went back to my trivial drawings thinking that when I finally interviewed for a job, I would be sure that it was a job waiting to be filled rather than a space just for appearance. I would look for a job description that said something besides, "take up space while the company bids on a contract to get work for its idle employees."

A phone call came one evening from Mr. Rhodes, head of the Boulder Unified School District, asking if I could teach a high-school drafting class the fall semester. I told him I might be interested, but unfortunately he took my response as a "Yes." Within two days I learned that all the college classes I needed for January graduation were offered that fall! The high school drafting class would conflict. Without me working, Phyllis and I decided we could ask for a loan from her folks so that I could finish school in January rather than extend until June. I called Mr. Rhodes to explain. He roared unkind words, stating that he already had processed the paperwork for me. The fact that I had not given him a positive "Yes" did not register with him. The conversation ended when he slammed his phone down. Ouch!

At that time companies visited the campus for job interviews. General Electric sent an offer for me to join their engineering training program in the Nuclear Energy Division. I could start in San Jose, California at $485/month. Based on today's wages, that would have been $5000/month! It took Phyllis and me about ten seconds to decide that we should accept the offer, and she mailed my acceptance letter the next morning. I would start February 1, 1958.

Phyllis's words keep coming back when I think about the collapse of my once secure drafting job at *Control Cells*. There was no panic or sign of distress when she said, "We don't have to worry about this!" She was confident then—she was right. The strength of her faith was greater than mine, and my faith began to grow in the realization that God was leading us through each day.

During the last semester, two professors asked me to be a grader for classes in fluid mechanics and heat transfer. It was a low-paying job, but helped pay for gas and groceries. It was a review since I had to work the homework and quizzes myself before I could grade the student's. That paid off later when I became an adjunct professor, teaching the same material at San Jose State University.

We asked Phyllis's folks for the loan when our account was gasping. They gladly helped us on our way to California. We loaded the 40 Chevy and began our journey west.

If I had known the following biblical truths, life could have been a steady stream of peaceful confidence instead of worrisome uncertainty.

Jesus said, "Peace I leave with you, My peace I give to you, not as the world gives do I give to you. Let not your heart be troubled, neither let it be afraid." (John 14:27)

And we know that all things work together for good to those who love God, to those who are the called according to His purpose. (Romans 8:28)

> The episodes described in this chapter suggest two questions a jobseeker could ask of an interviewer. One question: "Does the job consist of work where I can make a contribution?" A second question: "Is this job likely to involve a season of just occupying a work station or is there solid work to move this business forward?"

CHAPTER 26

CALIFORNIA HERE WE COME

Phyllis and I drove the southern route from Boulder in the '40 Chevy, loaded with everything we owned. The back seat was removed to make room for boxes. Whatever we couldn't fit inside or in the trunk we had wrapped in an orange canvas on the roof, tying it securely through the front and back windows. It took four days until we were finally on our way up from Los Angeles to San Jose where we found temporary lodging at the Pepper Tree Inn, directly across the street from General Electric. Phyllis was in her third month, expecting our first son. Being far away from home and friends was especially hard on her emotions.

I met Don the first day at GE, when he welcomed me into my first group and said, "You probably want to meet new friends. Let me invite you to church where we have a lot of them. There are young women who will make your wife feel like family." That was all it took. We met these warm-hearted people the following Sunday, and never had to search for friends after that. We had found a nice apartment by then and were getting settled.

General Electric (GE) had hired me and 19 other engineers for the *Advanced Engineering Program (AEP)* in San Jose, CA. The Program was one year of intense technical training to be followed by two years of management indoctrination to become *Top Brass Managers* in the Company. I survived the first year of weekly problem solving in the Nuclear Energy Department. We applied graduate level coursework to analyze existing problems, using mathematical techniques taught by GE experts and also guest professors from universities. Each of us wrote our own analysis reports while we worked at full-time job assignments. The first year was exhausting, but no one dropped out! I realized that I was in a group of high-achievers.

Everyone in the AEP was "pressured" to choose the second year indoctrination. We would relocate from San Jose to GE Aircraft Gas Turbines in Evendale, Ohio. I had to decide if I would continue with the AEP, or quit and settle for a local job assignment. Our Class Coordinator pushed the benefits of the AEP. As future managers we would have a furnished office and our own secretary. Our salary would increase to three times that of the average engineer. Tempting.

It was an easy decision for some members—a path to the top. Our Coordinator predicted a *gold-plated* future for those who continued the AEP, but I knew that nobody could predict the future and make such promises with absolute certainty. I couldn't know what would happen in the future until the future arrived. I was praying for weeks that God would show me what to do. Should I tell the Coordinator "Yes" or "No"? All other class members had decided to continue with the AEP. Today was the last day for me to decide.

During that first year with GE, Phyllis and I made friends with several people in the neighborhood who met every two weeks for potluck and a Bible study. The study was not put on by a church to recruit members. Its purpose was to "...see what's in the Book that we could use." People came from different backgrounds and no one promoted a personal agenda. It was assumed that if the Bible was a holy book as it claimed to be, it would contain ideas about how life should be lived for optimum effectiveness. That assumption fostered the motivation:

Look for Life Principles that can be applied to everyday affairs.

The group picked out a part of the Bible and someone volunteered to lead a discussion on it the following week. Interest grew as we discovered *life principles* during each session. Here's one I return to often:

Life Principle:
Trust in the Lord with all your heart, and lean not on your own understanding; in all your ways acknowledge Him, and He shall direct your paths. (Proverbs 3:5,6)

Concerning my present dilemma where I had to give a "Yes" or "No" to our Class Coordinator, I tried to *trust* and *acknowledge* God, waiting for His direction about which path to follow. There was silence. No sign. Maybe I could choose either path and it didn't matter to God. Either "Yes" or "No" was OK with Him. I said out loud so God would be sure to hear, "I'll tell the Coordinator 'Yes, I'll go on with the AEP.'" I was alone on the couch early that morning when I said that. Then something happened I never experienced before. I broke out in a drenching, cold sweat! I was dripping wet in less than a minute, and I hadn't moved a muscle! I said to God, "I think You are telling me I should say 'No.' Is that right?" The cold sweat stopped as fast as it came, and in several minutes I was dry! That's when I knew the right path—I knew the answer I should give.

I will remember that sweaty reaction as long as I live. It gave me confidence when I told our AEP Coordinator that I decided not to follow the AEP path. I expected one more "hard sell," explaining how I was choosing between being a "star" or a "nobody." But it wasn't like that. He was surprised and wondered why. I said I had no strong reason for deciding against it—the first year was a grand experience that would benefit my career. The main reason for not pursuing the AEP was that I believed God was guiding me in a different direction. When I described my sweaty answer to prayer, he listened carefully. He may have been thinking that GE wouldn't want a "religious nut" on their future management team, or he did not know how to refute my reasons. It's also possible he may have believed and understood me, but never disclosed his personal belief. He sighed and said, "I wish you the best. I would not argue with God." My friends from the AEP were on their way to "career success" as I settled into a Unit with a group of seasoned engineers. I never doubted my decision but had an increasing assurance that I was on the path God designed.

There was another *Life Principle* we discovered in the Bible:

Now to Him who is able to do exceedingly abundantly above all that we ask or think, according to the power that works in us, to Him

***be glory in the church by Christ Jesus to all generations, forever and ever. Amen. (**Ephesians 3:20, 21)*

I could not have anticipated how that principle would work out, but in summary: Within a year my boss urged me to enroll in the *Stanford Honors Cooperative Program*, attending daytime classes at the University several times a week. Seventeen years on the Program and many GE assignments later, I graduated with a PhD. In order to demonstrate Community involvement, GE volunteered me as a part-time Adjunct Professor when San Jose State University called for help in teaching overflow engineering students. That was a dream I held since college. Several of my graduate students became outstanding GE engineers. The years that followed my "cold sweat" decision showed me that God's path was fulfilling in ways I never imagined.

But, now back to the early years at GE:

One Best (?) Assignment

One of the best things (I thought) happened! I was assigned to Alan to do a four month work assignment. They said Al was a brilliant engineer so I thought he could teach me a lot. He did, but it was far from what I expected.

I moved to the empty desk in his cubicle and joined him at a table while he described my first problem. It was one that I knew I could work out, and it was a real problem! It didn't have a textbook solution. I eagerly went to work on it. By afternoon of the next day I had worked out a solution and written a short summary. Alan was surprised that I got through it so soon. I sat at the table as he read over each page of my summary, making marks with a red pen and mumbling to himself. When he finished with the last page, my summary had more red marks than my writing! He commented that I seemed to have made some wrong assumptions and did not include significant possibilities, but not to worry. He had another problem for me. I never did find out what was wrong with my first solution.

The second problem went the same way. It involved an interesting nuclear reactor flow network with malfunctioning valves that I could solve easily, and include other possible valve failures, but Alan bled all over my pages again and said my solution wouldn't work.

When he finished going over the third problem, he leaned back in his chair and said words that cut deeply:

"At last I thought I gave you something you could do, but I see I was wrong."

Those words, coming from the one whom I understood to be one of the most brilliant engineers in the department, stunned me. My importance, self-worth, and value were suddenly wiped out, leaving a shell of quivering, intense pain. I took my analysis off the table, turned around and sat at my desk in a stupor facing the wall for a long time wondering, "What Should I Do Now?"

I was ready to quit! But a verse from a recent noon-time Bible study stopped me:

And we know that all things work together for good to those who love God.. (Romans 8:28)

Where could I find any good from Alan's cutting words? If something good was supposed to come out of this low point in my life, whatever could it be? I asked God how He wanted me to respond. I don't hear ghostly voices. I believe God can lead a person by motivating his or her thoughts, and that must have been what happened next.

I knew about one problem in the nuclear safety industry: No one had found a way to predict how fast high-pressurized steam/water mixtures were expelled from pipe ruptures during postulated nuclear boiler accidents. They call it *blowdown*. If a pipe ruptures—how fast does the steam/water mixture come gushing out? There was plenty of experimental data, but from many attempts, there was still no theory to predict the discharge rates.

It was like one simple idea after another came into my mind, which I wrote down. Within a page and a half, I had a simple expression that predicted the *blowdown rate* that others had been trying to predict! It matched the available measurements! I couldn't hold it back and said, "Thank you, God!" Alan said, "What?" I replied, "I wasn't talking to you, Alan!" I grabbed up my *blowdown* analysis, rushed out of the cubicle to our big boss's office, and asked him for a minute of his time. When he saw my analysis and realized that my analysis predicted virtually all available data, he stood up and said,

"Write it up! Send it to the Society (an engineering society) for publication—I'll send you to a technical conference to present it! Alan's stuff can wait!"

Those words instantly restored my importance, self-worth, and value, which had been wiped away by Alan's words. They showed dramatically the power of words.

Surprisingly, Alan was happy for me! He even helped make reservations for the conference where I eventually presented the work, which became known as the "Moody Blowdown Model," and has been the nuclear industry safety standard for pipe-break accident analyses. God has a sense of humor in working things out on our lowest of low days.

Alan actually was an important *cog in the wheel*, to set the stage, or I might never have spent the down time at my desk writing the few short equations that became my *claim to fame*. Alan was not a bad guy—he was simply a perfectionist. No one could do his work to his satisfaction, no matter how perfect it was performed. He had to do it himself. The week after I was released from him to work on the "Moody Model" paper, three other engineers were assigned to him, and all three quit within a month. That's when management realized that Alan had to be an *individual contributor* without anyone working for him.

Many times I have been asked to speak about the "Moody Model" and other safety aspects of Nuclear Power plants. I always explain how God guided in formulating the model and how He works things out for good for those who love Him. But it doesn't stop there. He is ready to direct us in the most fulfilling path life has to offer.

Trust in the Lord with all your heart, and lean not on your own understanding; in all your ways acknowledge Him, and He shall direct your paths. (Proverbs 3:5,6)

Introduction to "Unholy Ground"

Phyllis and I had many new friends among the young couples that had made us part of their church family right away. After two years I was asked to be a member of the church deacon board without even knowing exactly what a deacon was. I accepted, seeing it would be with some of the older and wiser men in the church. Therefore, it had to be a safe commitment. They met monthly to discuss the physical, financial, and spiritual well-being of the church. At each meeting, I felt like I was in a circle of prophets, some with partly bald heads and grey beards. I saw them as older role models who would display their knowledge, understanding, and wisdom in solving any church problems that came to light. I was comfortable sitting quietly between two of them who were humble and smart.

One evening a discussion about the use of parking space went on for over an hour. We had numerous visitors and parking was a problem. It was friendly discussion with a lot of brainstorming. I had not voiced an opinion for my first six meetings because I felt inexperienced in the midst of the sages around me. But thinking of the church plot plan, and unused space, and how simple it would be to put up several signs directing traffic to the unused space, I saw how easily the parking problem could be solved. No one else saw the obvious, so I raised my hand to speak and described what I thought was a solution to the parking problem. The other deacons pondered it for 30 seconds. Mr. E., the

CEO of a large utility company serving the entire county, said, "That's the most stupid idea I ever heard!"

Silence. Ten deacons and I sat like statues. No one blinked! You could cut the air with a knife! Several began to shift in their chairs like adjusting for hemorrhoid discomfort, and a few pages were shuffled. The chairman cleared his throat and said, "Well, let's table that."

Nobody came to my rescue. Nobody dared to challenge Mr. E. for his words. He was a large financial supporter of the church and apparently everyone knew it. Later I thought about why no one challenged Mr. E.: "Heaven help the person who offends one who can cut off your lights and water if you offend him." But even in secular meetings, most people offer criticism with kind words to help someone improve. They don't generally chew them up and spit them out! The effect on me? I avoided Mr. E. for the next few years. It was six months before I worked up enough courage to make another suggestion. By that time, Mr. E.'s term on the board had expired and he was absent. I secretly forgave him, but I couldn't forget the incident. Whenever I think of it, the pain replays itself, although weaker. It turned out that someone else suggested the same solution I had proposed (*the most stupid idea*) and the Board bought it.

I wish I had been experienced like Senator George Vest, (1879-1903), who was once attacked in a stupid, irrational outburst. When the tirade ended, Vest rose and said, "Mr. President, after listening to the remarks of my learned colleague, I feel somewhat like the little corporal in the Philistine army who, after Samson had passed through, picked himself off the ground and, holding his battered head, cried out, 'Now I know what it feels like to be smitten by the jawbone of an ass.'"
(Humes, J. C., Podium Humor, Harper & Row, 1975, pg. 98)

With many years to think about it, I wish I had thought fast enough to say to Mr. E.,

"You know that I am the 'new kid on the block' and my thinking has not caught up with yours. I wanted to make a contribution with

what I thought might be a helpful idea, but according to Mr. E., it was a stupid idea. It will be a great help to me, Mr. E., if you will tell me exactly why it was the most stupid idea you ever heard. If I know what was stupid about it, I should be able to refine my future ideas. I am listening with both ears."

When someone says something that hurts me now, I don't suffer long-lasting pain like in earlier years. The reason is that today I am more confident of my abilities and I'm not afraid to agree if I'm wrong or if I make a stupid comment. Some wise person advised, *"If you're wrong, admit it. If you're right, shut up."*

You can't buy good advice like that! I admire anyone who is not afraid to admit their mistakes. It shows they are strong and don't have to manufacture excuses or blame someone else for their faults. If they are right and don't brag about it, they show humility in my view. I want to be like that.

Whenever we associate with others, someone is likely to say something that hurts. We should plan on it and be ready for it. It may occur when we and the other person are alone together. We can address his or her comment by saying we may not have understood them, and if we did, whatever they said hurt our feelings. Did they intend that? Then discuss it further. Did they have a valid point? Did they want to hurt us because we hold a view different from theirs? Does that make us poison on that point? In that case, it is best to avoid that point forever unless either of us changes our mind.

It also may turn out that what the other person said was not what he or she meant, and in no way did they intend to hurt us. They meant the opposite. A private talk can do *damage repair* at times like that. But we need to speak up.

There are likely to be times when someone says something that hurts us and others are present—that is, we have an audience made up of bystanders or interested people surrounding us, wondering how we are going to react. It's not easy to have a private conversation and settle the issue under a spotlight. That's one of those "What Should I do Now?" situations. Everyone knows the words spoken had to be painful.

There are times it is better to ignore what was said, which shows that you consider the comment beneath the dignity of the occasion, and will not glorify the cutting words or the speaker by addressing them. There are other times where it would be better to let our *audience* know about our reaction. We could respond like, "Ouch! I see that I pressed a hot button!" and then admit that it is OK to disagree. You can always confess to the one who said the cutting words, "You know, you could be way ahead of me on this. Give me some time to catch up and see if I still have an opposing view. I just ask one small favor—please don't hate me if I fail to see things exactly like you do." Then change the subject.

A soft answer turns away wrath, but a harsh word stirs up anger. The tongue of the wise uses knowledge rightly, but the mouth of fools pours forth foolishness. (Proverbs 15: 1, 2)

> Remember when someone said something that hurt you deeply. What did you do then? If it happened now, would you react differently? Why?

CHAPTER 27

HOW DO YOU FIX THAT?

My 1940 Chevy had reached its last mile, and repairs would cost more than the car was worth. A junk dealer claimed extraordinary generosity by paying $7.00 for it, and we watched sorrowfully as he towed it away. But now we had a used '53 Chevy sedan.

We had begun our two-week vacation from San Jose, where I worked at the GE Nuclear Energy Department and Phyllis was a full-time Mom and homemaker. This was our third day of travel, marking the three-quarters point to get to our hometown, Aurora, Illinois. Grandparents would be waiting like vultures to snatch up their grandson, David, for the first time. It was a quiet ride because he slept most of the time between baby food snacks in his port-a-crib that fit in the back seat.

The scenery looked like picture postcards of cornfields, red barns and farmhouses against blue sky and puffy white clouds. Suddenly, the car jerked like the engine had stopped briefly. Nothing seemed to be wrong, and I thought it must have been a bump in the highway. After an hour it happened again. Then it did it twice in a row. It was not bumps in the road. "What Should I Do Now?" I wondered. I hoped that car trouble wouldn't ruin our vacation.

I checked the gas gage and the tank was half full. An hour later the car jerked a few more times. When I stopped for gas, I asked a mechanic for his opinion. He checked under the hood, examined the carburetor and spark plug connections, and didn't see anything wrong. He thought it might be a burned valve, but that would give a regular jerk. Then he thought there might be dirt in the gas tank.

When the sun was getting low in the sky, Phyllis said, "That looks like a good place." We pulled into a rest stop. I carried our Coleman stove and ice chest from the trunk to a picnic table while Phyllis changed an overdue diaper for our one-year-old passenger. I fired up the stove and Phyllis made hamburgers (after scrubbing our son and her hands).

We could afford low-budget motels and simple meals by cooking eggs and making sandwiches. As long as the engine misfire remained intermittent, we could reach our home town and have a garage check it later.

I didn't sleep much our last night on the road, worrying if the car would actually get us home. If the engine misfiring got worse, it might stop. I asked God to keep it running until we got to Phyllis's house. The next morning after having some corn flakes on our tailgate, we started the car and were on our last 300 miles. There was no engine cutting out for two hours, and then it began. God did not *heal* our car, but He was answering my prayer. We pulled into the driveway of Phyllis's folks in the late afternoon. I remember cheers and open arms.

The rest of the day was chaotic with grandparents and relatives grabbing the newest member of the family. The big problem was trying to get him away from the grandparents for another diaper change, but that was the least of their priorities. My solution was to hand one of them a diaper and then disappear into the crowd. Phyllis would not go along with my idea. They had determined not to let him go until they all got a piece of him. Finally it was time for the family potluck to start. It was the first opportunity to discuss the car problem with Phyllis's brother, Paul. He could repair anything, and would help me fix the problem in the morning.

The next morning, Paul and I agreed with the opinion I first got from the mechanic that the symptoms pointed to dirt in the gas tank. I jacked up the rear end of the car and was beginning to unfasten the metal straps holding the tank while Paul was snooping under the hood. He called, "Hey! Come look at this!" I wriggled out from under the car.

He was pointing to something. "That wire is loose! I think that must be the problem!" We were staring at the distributor which sends an electric jolt to each spark plug so that they spark at the right time, burn the gas in the cylinders, and drive the engine. But a wire is attached to the outside of the distributor shell that delivers electric current to fire the spark plugs. The loose wire was ready to fall off. If it came off, there would be no spark, and the engine would not run. Paul tightened the screw that held the wire, and the problem was fixed! The engine never misfired again! The engine misfire acted like a *decoy* with symptoms of dirt in the gas tank, and I almost removed the gas tank to fix the loose wire problem!

Other times, either I or someone I knew was fixing a problem that turned out to be a *decoy*. That is, it wasn't the actual problem. Not only were time, resources, and money wasted, but the problem continued to do its damage, causing continued loss.

Symptoms, Wrong Assumptions, and Loss Caused by Another Decoy

I remember another time when an inventor thought a problem could not be fixed, and that almost led to the destruction of a remarkable invention. It started when a former boss called and asked if I would talk with a lawyer about getting a patent for a small air conditioner. The device was only as big as a toaster and used air instead of freon. It would cost one-tenth the price of an automobile air conditioner, and it could cool spaces larger than an automobile. It was invented in his client's garage.

He was a hands-on Japanese inventor, not an engineer, who *played* in his garage and sometimes *lucked out* with a useful idea like the Bic Lighter years before. The lawyer realized the dollar value of his newest *plaything* and wanted an expert to determine its validity. I was happy to be the one.

The inventor gave me his sketches with English details, after I signed a confidentiality agreement. I analyzed the theoretical aspects and was dumbfounded! He had built a small air conditioner with a series of connected pipes, mini-compressors, mini-pumps, expansion chambers, and coolers that took in room temperature air and discharged cold air. It took no more power than an auto heater. It was unlike any device I had ever seen advertised or in practice. Both he and the lawyer were happy to get my report.

The lawyer had arranged for several reps from the auto industry to visit the inventor's garage for a demonstration. The plan was that the automotive industry would secure the patent and rights to manufacture and sell the device, but the inventor would retain ownership.

The inventor asked me to check out his demonstration model in Ontario, California. When I flew there from San Jose, he was despairing. The demonstration was running, the discharging air was cold, but the registered temperature showed it was warm. Nothing he tried fixed the problem. The automakers would believe only the measurement, and the measurement showed the device was not producing cold air. It was not what he had claimed.

The inventor was defeated, and was picking up the phone to call off the demonstration. He was planning to tear down his model and forget the entire project. Then I saw something! "Don't call it off! Look here!" He came over reluctantly.

All thermometers for incoming air and one of the two discharges were labeled "°C." The discharge instrument he had been watching was labeled "°F." It should have been a Celsius or Centigrade thermometer like the others, but instead it had a Fahrenheit scale. When he changed the thermometer to read Centigrade, results matched his claims.

The inventor was going to destroy his model and either rebuild it or junk it by trusting the *decoy* temperature measurement. The actual problem was that he was reading data from a *decoy* thermometer with the wrong temperature scale. He solved the real problem by changing the thermometer to one with the correct scale.

> *Through wisdom a house is built, and by understanding it is established; by knowledge the rooms are filled with all precious and pleasant riches. A wise man is strong, yes, a man of knowledge increases strength; for by wise counsel you will wage your own war, and in a multitude of counselors there is safety."* **(Proverbs 24: 3-6)**

Both the distributor loose wire and the wrong thermometer episodes, as well as the Proverb above, show me that we should ask one or more persons to examine what we are thinking, doing, or planning because they likely will have a point of view different from ours. They may see obvious pitfalls, or recognize a *decoy*, or even opportunities that we overlook.

> Did you ever fix a "non-problem" after you carefully diagnosed the trouble? Who would you trust to tell you if a problem is physical, psychological, or spiritual in nature?

CHAPTER 28

WHO AM I ?

I remember stopping to see what the excitement was on my way to class during my senior year in high school. Kids were swarming someone in the hallway. It was Eugene, a *wallflower*, not outgoing or friendly—a typical *nobody* in those days. Today he had a big smile. Then I learned why.

Eugene had just received his driver's license! His wealthy parents let him drive the family car to school and kids could ride with him! At that time, the few students who drove cars enjoyed *god-like status,* and Eugene had transfigured overnight to the holy corridors of the "most esteemed" of the senior class! I am sure I became his passenger more than a few times. His life had changed instantly by the small plastic license he displayed in his wallet. He also had the keys and a car at his disposal.

I understand now, after many years, Eugene had a serious, problem. It had nothing to do with my being jealous of his sudden rise in popularity above mine because I didn't have a car. I didn't have enough psychological smarts to put a name on Eugene's problem, but I bet there was a non-pronounceable medical name for it. I don't think Eugene could have known he had the problem, but I have seen it other times in others besides Eugene. It destroyed friends I have known—people I have worked with! I call it a *personal identity* problem. You don't have to be a psychology major to diagnose it. In street language, you can describe it by the question, "Who am I?" Auxiliary questions are, "Who do my friends think I am?" or, "Who do I think I am?"

Overnight Eugene was transformed from being a *nobody* to being a *star!* He had a car, and now he was everyone's cherished friend and chauffeur. He always had a company of kids to go with him to hamburger drive-ins, to a game, to a party, or just to cruise with the windows down. Having a friend with a car gave kids temporary status! Eugene was *Mr. Popular Guy* with an automobile. It was the car that gave him *his identity*—like a guy in a gorilla costume who began to think he was a gorilla with all the rights and privileges of a gorilla! I thought, "If Eugene lost the car, he would be *Mr. Nobody* again." That was when I realized *If your identity is based on something you can lose, you are living on dangerous ground.*

Most of my friends had their own *identities*, based on *who they were*, not on who they imagined they were or something they possessed. They were well-known for *something they could do*. The parents of another student, Bob, belonged to the swank Aurora Country Club, and Bob could swim in the pool any time without charge. He could also bring his friends! His identity could be *"Mr. Freestyle."* He had dozens of friends who followed him through the guard-gate several times each week during the hot summer. Other boys were good in sports. Their identity was defined by what they did best. *"Mr. Bulldozer"* would apply to the star fullback, *"Mr. Glue-hands"* for the guy who caught touchdown passes, *"Miss Loud mouth"* for the head cheerleader. They were known as *stars*. I made fireworks and small firecrackers with my chemistry set and was known as *"Mr. Bomb Maker."*

All of us participated in games and other class activities making many friends apart from our specific *identities*. Socially, we were on a first-name basis with our circle of friends. If one of us needed help, the rest of us came to aid.

Fast forward to my engineering career where I knew two brilliant men. Jim was a pump expert and Don was a valve expert. Nuclear power plants need dozens of pumps and valves of all kinds and sizes, and these experts knew everything about their product. Both pumps and valves can be as big as a five-story parking garage or small enough to fit in your nose. They knew all the brands and specifications. They were walking, breathing product catalogues.

Mr. Pump Man

I could go to Jim's cubicle to ask him for specifications of any given pump design. He would turn his swivel chair to one of the three bookshelves covering the walls of his office, filled with catalogues and data-binders, and retrieve one. In a moment, he had the page open to the exact information I needed. "Mr. Pump Man" was Jim's identity for years. The day came for Jim to retire. Most people looked forward to retirement. Not Jim, but it was mandatory. He went home and ceased communication with his former associates. His wife complained that Jim felt like he had no value anymore. He had no purpose in life. His identity was lost. Jim purchased a revolver and killed his wife and himself. *It was a tragedy of one who let his identity be something he could lose.*

Mr. Valve Man

Don also had a cubicle library of valves—small and large. He, too, could find specifications on any valve that was made—the opening and closing times, flow rate, and necessary power to operate them. Another GE downsizing came, and forced retirement for Don. He became a recluse at home for six months before killing himself. He was another man who lost his identity, and thereafter believed that he had no value or purpose, no reason to go on living.

Dr. Physicist Par Excellence

My close friend Bob was a brilliant physicist, employed many years by a research lab in the Bay Area. His technical contributions and patents set him apart as *one of the best*, working under intense pressure often to be *first in technical breakthroughs*. He received many honors, well-deserved fame, and much exposure in the high-tech world.

People enjoyed Bob's dry sense of humor, like the time he told one of his bald colleagues the latest theory on natural hair color. With a straight face and his most serious tone, he said, "When the hair follicles penetrate the scalp and work their way through the skull, if they contact grey matter, you'll have grey or black hair. If they contact white brain cells, you have white hair. (Bob's hair at the time had turned white.) If the follicles don't contact anything in your head, you end up bald."

His wife, Dottie, shared the spotlight with Bob as his supportive wife and helpmate. When mandatory retirement came, they had to say *goodbye!* to the rewarding high-tech, high-visibility life they had enjoyed, and they transitioned to an entirely different world in the gold-rush town of Murphys, California.

New activities for Bob and Dottie included volunteering as docents for Murphy's Museum and joining the San Andreas Television staff to learn the broadcasting business. They learned video production and later produced a weekly "Armchair Video Travelogue" for residents of their retirement village. They inspired others who had lost or misplaced their identities at retirement. By their example, they helped people find a *new identity* in serving others with their particular talents and abilities.

When Dottie died, Bob didn't have to ask, "What Should I Do Now?" He continued to produce Armchair Travel Videos for many who would never visit the faraway lands. "Of course I miss her beyond words," he confessed. "But it's comforting that we both know our destination." He often would recite a Bible verse that brought him comfort, like this one:

Jesus said, "Let not your heart be troubled; you believe in God, believe also in Me. In My Father's house are many mansions; if it were not so, I would have told you. I go to prepare a place for you. And if I go and prepare a place for you, I will come again and receive you to Myself; that where I am, there you may be also. (John 14:1-3)

Let's go back to the title of this chapter: *Who am I?* Some have rightly called themselves "a work in progress." Where should I begin to look for the answer to who I am?

Blessed is the man who walks not in the counsel of the ungodly, nor stands in the path of sinners, nor sits in the seat of the scornful, but his delight is in the law of the Lord, and in His law he meditates day and night. He shall be like a tree planted by the rivers of water, that brings forth its fruit in its season, whose leaf also shall not wither; and whatsoever he does shall prosper.
(Psalm 1: 1-3)

Jesus said, "I am the vine, you are the branches. He who abides in Me, and I in him, bears much fruit; for without Me you can do nothing." (John 15:5)

...With God all things are possible. (Matthew 19:26b)

> People want to change their appearance, strength, expertise, or other characteristics if they are unhappy about themselves. They may want to hide behind a more admirable identity. I confess that I have done that. Maybe you have, too. Would you call it normal, abnormal, or something to be fixed?

CHAPTER 29

THE NOT-SO-FAIR WORLD'S FAIR

It was 11 PM when we arrived in Knoxville. My second oldest son, John, had driven our station wagon most of the way with his younger brother, Paul as "co-pilot", while Phyllis and I enjoyed riding in the back seat and our youngest son, Dan lounged on a sleeping bags in the rear cargo area. We were looking for an address to the house where we would spend the next two days. This was probably our last road trip vacation with John since he would be starting school on the East Coast. Our oldest son, Dave, was missing because he was already attending the police academy. "There it is!" one of them shouted, pointing to a small, white house.

We had driven from home in California over the last week, stopping to see grandparents in Illinois while "motel-camping" along the way, but this would be a special vacation, I thought—*The 1982 World's Fair!* Phyllis's *Good Housekeeping* magazine ran an ad for houses in Knoxville that families were renting to visitors coming to the fair. I sent money to rent this house for two days. It was suited for a family of six, walking distance to the fair, and it came with kitchen privileges.

We parked in the driveway, and I retrieved the rental agreement. The house was dark, but the instructions listed a phone number to get the key. We found a pay phone nearby. The phone number they gave was disconnected! John shined a flashlight through the windows. The house was empty! No furniture—no rugs—no appliances. A light was on at the house next door. The neighbor said that the residents had moved out long ago and the house was a bank repo. We had been scammed. "What Should I Do Now?"

We were dog-tired, so we looked for a motel. Our favorite and *most economical* chain was full, and so were all the surrounding motels because of the Fair. But the receptionist was understanding and telephoned to help us find the closest vacancy. It was a one-hour drive out of Knoxville! When we arrived, we fell into bed, too exhausted to be angry.

The next morning, we walked next door to a highway cafe' for breakfast. Pancakes, eggs, bacon, waffles, corn flakes, and coffee lifted our spirits after a disappointing evening. We couldn't have been the only ones who paid rental money to a bogus agency that disappeared with all the cash gotten by cheating people. There was nothing we could do to right the wrong. We had to swallow hard and take the loss. However, our family discussion was priceless when we considered what God says in the Bible about how He wants us to react when we have been robbed—when we want to somehow get revenge:

> *…Do not avenge yourselves, but rather give place to wrath; for it is written, "Vengeance is Mine, I will repay," says the Lord. (***Romans 12:19)**

It was consoling to understand that God knew who stole from all who were conned by the *Good Housekeeping* ad. Whatever we have belongs to Him, and in a true sense, the thieves stole from God. We can release it and not let it affect or infect our time together.

We drove back to the fair and paid the huge admission price. *Energy Turns the World***,** was the exciting theme and we were eager to see the displays that were advertised as the most amazing ever created by science. We hurried past huge, boring posters lining the midway, that would have taken hours to read, on our way to the demonstration area. We found large, temporary buildings that housed scheduled presentations.

These were the *must see* attractions. Blocking the entrance to each attraction was a ticket booth! Whopping ticket prices! There was no warning. My heart sank. Embarrassed, I had to tell my sons I did not plan on these high prices for each attraction. They understood. I had a credit card, but we had determined to pay cash for everything. We started out with $1200 in traveler's checks we had saved during the year for this trip to cover motels, restaurants, gasoline, and other expenses, so there wasn't enough for the expensive fair attractions. We bought high-priced sandwiches and cold drinks, ate at a table under a shade tree, and then left Knoxville.

No one could have predicted the lasting effect of our round-trip cross-country drive. It was *motel camps*, hamburger and hot dog cookouts with a Coleman stove at rest stops, and cozy roadside restaurant stops, all with the family *tuning-in* to each other. The long-term results have helped us all to remain close even though our sons' interests vary widely from law enforcement and audio/video technology to high-energy particle physics. The minor disappointments like the house-rental scam and *insufficient funds* at the World's Fair shrink to the size of a mosquito bite compared to the bonding road-trip memories that will last a lifetime.

I believe that we are *wired* for close relationships. There seems to be worldly efforts to destroy the concept and need for family, but that is like trying to destroy our need for air. We need the closeness of others to live as God created us in His image. To those who are blessed with a traditional family as we were, the love of Christ can abound when the members have entrusted their lives to Him. Phyllis, my wife of 59 years and the mother of our four sons, was a channel of His love. Since she died, what they miss most is the way Phyllis let God's love generously wash over them throughout their lives. I, too, was such a beneficiary. We can readily join the chorus of Proverbs, which says,

Her children rise up and call her blessed: Her husband also, and he praises her: **(Proverbs 31:28)**

We are thankful that she knew her eternal destination (where there could be no bank repos) and she made certain that we knew ours.

> Suppose you were robbed by an ad or other appeal from a leading resource with a good reputation. You invested and lost with no hope for recovery, and you are asking, "What Should I do now?" Did you come up with workable options? Was this just a "lesson learned" incident which left you wiser, and likely more skeptical?

CHAPTER 30

INDIA

I grabbed my suitcase from the conveyor belt at the Delhi airport and followed non-verbal signs to the taxi lines. It was midnight on New Year's Eve after a flight from San Francisco with a plane change in London. After 20 hours in the air, I thought I could last one more hour for a cab ride and hotel check-in before finally falling onto a soft bed!

"Taxi, mister?" A young man stepped out of the shadows and said he operated a van service with cheaper fares than taxis. "I know shortcuts and get you to hotel faster than taxi." I followed him to his *van*, a patched-up station wagon. He put my luggage in the back seat and I climbed in next to it.

We had driven a half-mile from the airport on a dark road when he pulled off the road and said, "Gas tank low. No money. You give me money for gas." I knew then the guy was a crook. He had to know that people arriving late at night would be tired and fall for his game. He would probably inflate the fare to the hotel also.

I think my normal reaction would have been a soft but firm request to take me back to the airport because I was not going to pay for gas or any other items he might tack on to his services. Since I am a Christian, I try to put the brakes on my mouth and avoid saying what I feel like saying because it wouldn't be nice and might do harm. But there are those times when *the holy glow begins to go!* I was tired and angry, and not in a mood to score Good Samaritan points! My inflamed patience won and I threw open the back door. Pulling out my luggage, I said, "You are a crook, and so I am walking back to the airport to get an honest cab driver—someone I can trust." He protested, and said he would take me directly to the hotel. (At least he must have wanted the fare.)

In fifteen minutes, we arrived at the hotel where a bellman greeted me. The *van* driver said the fare would be 21 U.S dollars. I asked the bellman what the normal cab fare was from the airport. He said seven instead of 21. I gave the *van* driver seven and walked away to shouts of nasty names and curses in perfect English. Someone had informed me that the dominant religion in India was Hinduism. When you die, you come back in a new life form which depends on how well you lived your previous lives. If bad, you might be a leper. If good, you might be a wealthy business man or princess. If more bad than good, you might be a thief like the taxi driver. Hotel check-in was fast and the bed was soft. The next thing I knew it was mid-morning.

I remembered my "welcome to India" experience the night before. No one had cautioned me to beware of thieves and robbers, but there were good indications to be on the lookout. I had done safety analysis for the Tarapur Atomic Power Station (TAPS) in India, a boiling water nuclear reactor designed by General Electric. Construction of the plant had suffered numerous delays because components containing copper were regularly stolen from the site to be sold on the black market. Transformers, tubing, switchgear, and wires had to be ordered and re-ordered to combat the thievery, with a cumulative construction delay of a year. Thievery of all kinds was how a segment of the population survived economically. I should have suspected the one-of-a-kind *van* driver before climbing into his *van*.

I missed a simple warning from Proverbs, or I wouldn't have been "taken for a ride" :

Where there is no counsel, the people fall; but in the multitude of counselors there is safety. (Proverbs 11:14)

I had not asked anyone about the credibility of this driver who came out of the shadows. He was not part of the mainstream taxi service. It was my fault for not getting information on such an independent courier.

There was another warning I missed. I could not claim being too tired to care, because that would have been a lame excuse.

He who is slow to anger is better than the mighty. And he who rules his spirit than he who takes a city. **(Proverbs 16:12)**

I had failed! My anger had taken over with the van driver. Later I did feel bad enough to ask God to forgive me since I had lost it. I sensed God's response, "Yes, you did, and that's why I died for you—and the van driver, too. It's good you didn't tell him you were a Christian! It would have driven him further away from Me!" I can't think of more fitting words that describe my feelings other than, "Damn my big mouth!" Even when I'm tired, I still have to learn to bite my tongue!

And the tongue is a fire, a world of iniquity. The tongue is so set among our members that it defiles the whole body, and sets on fire the course of nature; and it is set on fire by hell. For every kind of beast and bird, of reptile and creature of the sea, is tamed and has been tamed by mankind. But no man can tame the tongue. It is an unruly evil, full of deadly poison. With it we bless our God and Father, and with it we curse men, who have been made in the similitude of God. Out of the same mouth proceed blessing and cursing. My brethren, these things ought not to be so. **(***James 3:6-10***)**

The phone rang. "Fred! This is John L., University of Houston. Can you meet in the lobby for breakfast?" I didn't know John was attending the same conference! We met for an American breakfast and learned that we could hire a city taxi for $35. all day to show us around. It was an inexpensive way to have a private sightseeing tour. We met a friendly yellow cab driver at noon.

The driver pointed out important sights in Delhi. Part of the city included stunning architecture, brightly colored structures, glistening walkways, fountains, benches, flower gardens, and parks. Another part of the city was shocking! Beautiful homes, apartments, yards, playgrounds, and manicured properties were on one side of the street. Directly across the street was a human wasteland with crumbling shacks, lean-to shelters, broken benches, cluttered yards, garbage heaps, community water troughs, and push-carts. The driver noted that the rich section housed those who had lived good lives in the past, and the slum section housed those who had lived bad lives or were trying to better themselves for the next life.

He drove out of town to a small village with huts made of dried mud and grass. We saw a community water well and people filling jars. No garbage was in sight and barefoot children were running, laughing, playing tag or kicking a ball on the dusty ground. The driver proudly told us it was where he lived. This village was like a well-kept resort compared to the human zoo a few streets before.

Shortly after leaving his village, he drove to an isolated area. There was a large hill with many carved ledges. "When someone dies, we place their body on one of those ledges," he said. "Why?" John asked. The driver silently pointed to the top of a hill where we could see a company of the ugliest looking vultures perched. Large yellow beaks, evil-penetrating eyes, reddish throats textured like grape-clusters, huge black bodies, and razor-like claws, waiting for the next feast. After numerous rebirths, the Hindus teach, if the progression improves each time, a person may reach Nirvana, the highest and permanent life form. Disposing of a body with the help of vultures is merely a housekeeping task.

Our bodies return to dirt eventually. Most of us don't talk about it much, but it is a reality. I had a neighbor who wanted to be buried under her rosebushes so she could "come forth as a blooming rose." She was saying that she wanted to be fertilizer! Whether fertilizer or vulture poop, it doesn't matter to the deceased.

In some villages of India, if the husband dies, the practice of *sati* was in force from the 1500s where they placed his body on a stack of firewood to reduce him to ashes, and his wife was placed alongside him while she was still living and they both *went up in smoke* together. At first it was considered honorable for the wife to throw herself on the bonfire to remain true to her husband in the next life. Later it was an enforced practice. At last in 2015, the practice was made illegal throughout India, even though it occurs occasionally.

We have the option of being reduced to bone powder and ashes via cremation, but only after being pronounced dead. A policeman told of a widow who placed an ad begging the thief who stole her husband's ashes to return them. Within a week she found a corpse on her front porch with bullet holes in his chest. Her husband's urn was tied around his neck with a note that read, *"Here are your husband's ashes. Sorry we started to snort them. This is the thief that stole them and tried to pedal them as dope."* (I couldn't verify this exact news item from a newspaper or computer search. It came via law enforcement from unofficial police buzz. There are numerous internet reports of people snorting cremated human and animal remains by accident, supporting its integrity.)

Before we drove to the country, we were waiting for a stoplight at a busy intersection. It was early afternoon and getting warm, so the windows were open. John and I were trying to keep cool in the back seat, hoping the light would change so some air would circulate, when we were suddenly shocked. A beggar in a white robe had come to the driver's side and reached both arms into the back seat for a handout. We were immediately looking at two arms with two stumps without hands. He kept appealing in words we couldn't understand. His slim, bearded face was anguished. The driver repeated something to him and he turned away as traffic started to move. "Probably was caught stealing," said the driver.

I was thinking, "So they cut off your hands for stealing? That would probably reduce thievery more effectively than taking the robber to jail, scolding him, and turning him loose after giving him back his gun like we do in some states. Then, again—the poor man might have been a leper or the victim of a terrible accident. Not knowing the whole story, we have the built-in tendency to draw our own conclusions, right or wrong.

After seeing a few more sights, our driver drove us to Agra to see the Taj Mahal. Its beauty leaves some onlookers gasping! The structure is a mausoleum built in 1638 by Shah Jahan to memorialize his wife, Mumtaz Mahal, who died in childbirth. The four supporting pillars slope outward in case of an earthquake. That way, only outdoor visitors will get smashed but the inside furniture will be spared. The breathtaking sight was distracted by devilish little monkeys that run loose and torment tourists. They are the same species you see with organ grinders, running around with a tin cup for donations from the crowd and they piss on you if you fail to donate. Sometimes at the Taj they bite and steal purses and other articles! One of them attacked a woman's hat with a fruit basket decoration while we were there! They are a protected species and you can't hurt them. They know it, too, which makes them bolder!

It finally occurred to me that they protect these monkeys because they may be someone coming up from a past life! We had to give them every chance to get a better deal in the next cycle of life! With apologies to monkey lovers, I suggest sending them on their way to the next cycle. Bring on the starving pit bulls! They have to be at least one advanced cycle up and they don't steal purses—although they bite!

I don't remember anything about the nuclear conference that took me to India, but the guided tour gave me a contrast of colorful scenery and filthy surroundings. I felt *alone* with the people, culture, behavior, customs, morals, and rituals, some of which were shockingly different and repulsive. When people from India visit America for the first time, they probably feel the same way. I saw that people live according to *what they believe*. If we are born into a certain *belief system* and we claim it for our own, then we live according to what that system teaches. The differences between people group beliefs can lead to conflicts, fighting, and wars. The hate, grief, and pain that follow are traceable to what people believe. "What Shall I Do Now?" Biblical faith offers an answer:

Be anxious for nothing, but in everything by prayer and supplication, with thanksgiving, let your requests be made known to God; and the <u>peace of God</u>, which surpasses all understanding, will guard your hearts and minds through Christ Jesus.
(Philippians 4: 6,7)

> Most people believe a certain way and that way governs the way they live. That was obvious from what I saw in India. If someone wants to know what is the true faith to follow, do you have an answer?

CHAPTER 31

AN IMPORTANT VISITOR

It was almost quitting time and the boss knocked at the open side of my office cubicle. None of the cubicles had swinging doors in the spacious warehouse facility, and he was already parking himself on my visitor's chair. "Are you in tomorrow?" I tried to anticipate his next question and was wondering, "What Should I Do Now?" Before any excuse popped up into my mind, I told him, "Yes." He went on to say that his daughter's class was having a "go to work with dad day." His daughter would be coming to work with him to see what he did. As a manager, he didn't think his job would be interesting to such a young person. I could almost read his mind at that point.

Some of the dads had exciting jobs. When the teacher asked the kids to tell what they learned about their fathers' jobs, he could imagine one student telling about the big, red fire truck his dad rode on to put out fires. Another student would describe what it felt like to ride around the city in a police car with her dad. Someone else would describe the huge, noisy machines that bent big metal bars in a factory, and another would tell how her dad gave shots to help sick animals get well. My boss would only have an enclosed cubicle with several filing cabinets, a large table and chairs, a desk, and telephone. That wasn't much for a young daughter to brag about in school. The reason became clear why he showed up in my cubicle. "Do you suppose you could tell Monica the kind of work you do as one of our team members?" he asked. "It is much more dramatic than the paper shuffling and conducting meetings that I do." He was asking me to entertain and impress his daughter with spectacular assignments I had worked on. I said I would be glad to talk with her.

WHAT SHOULD I DO NOW?

My boss brought his daughter, Monica, to my cubicle the next morning for a proper introduction and left her. I could tell she was surprised at the size and simplicity of my 12-by-12 cubicle, probably because her father had described me to her with generous words of praise that, in her mind, should have merited a plush office with windows overlooking a gorgeous landscape. But I diverted her attention to some colored pictures of reactors and containment systems I had placed on the table.

Monica hung on to every word as I described accidents that could happen in nuclear power plants and the inventions we had developed to prevent those accidents from harming anyone. We talked about all imaginable accidents, including high-pressure pipe ruptures, steam explosions, earthquakes and flooding damage, terrorist attacks, and airplane crashes into nuclear power plants. She asked questions that were thoughtful and showed a depth of understanding that is lacking even in adults. I realized soon that I was in a conversation with a young mind of great potential.

The phone rang. I said to Monica, "Pardon me just a moment," and picked it up. It was a customer who should have contacted the boss, but he bypassed him and was anxious to get a status on his job that I was working on. The boss could have told him that it would be on time, and this was an unnecessary interruption. Monica heard me tell the caller, "I'm in a very important meeting now. I'll have to call you later today." I hung up and turned back to my young visitor. "That was a customer. We told him several days ago that we would have his job ready on time." I held up a manila folder with his job in it. "I guess he doesn't trust us, or he just wanted to be sure we didn't forget him. We never forget anybody." Then Monica and I went back to our discussion of nuclear accidents and safety systems.

Some years after I retired, I enjoyed a few minutes with my former GE boss at a reunion. He told me that Monica had become a practicing surgeon and a clinical associate professor at Stanford Hospital.

Furthermore, she was married, and she had a baby boy and a baby girl. I got to see pictures of the grandchildren! My boss also told me something that made me freeze for a moment. He said that Monica often tells her version of the "going to work with dad" story using my exact words, "I'm in a very important meeting now." She couldn't believe I said that—that I thought she was so important! She says she still can't believe it! But it apparently warms her heart to occasionally play those words over in her mind.

It is sobering to realize how the things we say when young people hear us can make a significant impression or long-term effect on them that we don't foresee at the time.

Pleasant words are like a honeycomb, sweetness to the soul and health to the bones. (Proverbs 16:24)

> Did you ever say something that was overheard by someone you did not realize was within hearing distance? Later they recited your quote to you or someone else as a statement that affected them for good or otherwise. How did you feel about that?

CHAPTER 32

PROFESSOR: ROLE MODELS

This was my first semester as an adjunct professor of engineering at San Jose State. My previous "professor experiences" were as a student, trying to learn whatever the professors were teaching. Each professor had an attribute that showed what made him or her an *outstanding* or *not-so-good* teacher—in my opinion. As a new adjunct I had to be myself, but I also wanted to have a teaching approach that embraced the outstanding attributes of the professors that inspired me.

My long-range hope to teach college students had now become a reality. It was natural to remember professors that scored high on my *admiration scale* and low on my *toxic* or *poisonous scale* when it came to teaching. By now I had a collection of professors who were role-models of the two extremes:

Virgil B. (V. B.) was a cheerful professor at Blackburn, my first college. The class came alive when he entered wearing his sly smile. He started each math class, with a twinkle in his eye, to get us ready for a surprise. He often jolted us with a puzzle or startling mathematical truth that seemed impossible—until he proved it! It was the most refreshing class I took at this small liberal arts college in Southern Illinois where we worked half time for the school and attended classes half time. *V. B.* laughed a lot and made mathematics fun, like the time he called out one part of a parabola known as "the latus-rectum." He said, with a straight face, "It was not to be confused with the tail end of the digestive tract...!" We looked forward to his morning class. I wanted my students to look forward to my classes.

We could expect the exact opposite from *John S. (J. S.)*, a chemistry professor also at Blackburn, who stood stiff in front of the classroom, wearing the same wrinkled suit and tie every day for weeks! No one got close enough to check his breath or deodorant. He resembled a propped-up corpse who droned on and on in a monotone for 50 minutes, much like a ventriloquist's dummy. His mouth opened and closed, revealing leftover traces of lunch still in the corners. His eyes blinked occasionally when he looked up from his notes. He didn't ask questions or provide opportunities for class interaction. The ending bell was a wake-up call for many students. After the bell, he referred all questions to his lab assistant, who stood by his side during his lecture, probably to steady him if he tipped over. I learned this from Professor *J. S.: putting students to sleep with a boring lecture could never be an option for me.*

A Denver lawyer, *Paul D. (P. D.)*, taught a summer course in business law, required for engineers at the University of Colorado. Every weekday I joined eleven students, seated on one side of a long table with case books open in front of us. Fast-talking *P. D.* sat on the other side in a swivel chair so he could instantly make eye contact with any one of us. It was a threatening "courtroom terror environment." We studied several legal cases each evening and had to be ready for oral quizzing the next day. *P. D.* skipped any warm greeting to the class. He sat down, scanned our tense faces, and began: "In the case of Lyons vs. Ford Motors, what was the complaint—Arthur?" Arthur squirmed, stuttered, and tried to squeak out an answer. "The rule of law was—Sherman?" Sherman nearly choked and tried to catch his breath. But before he could answer, P. D. pounced again—"William?" By then William had composed an answer and Arthur was still wondering what happened. It was nail-biting torture—high-pressure training, gut-wrenching fast-thinking answers. Letting the class know what was expected was a good thing.

For my own teaching, I would want to let students know they should adjust their own goals and know the subject so well that they could answer any and all anticipated questions. This would prepare them for those important meetings to answer questions which would undoubtedly come from their big boss someday.

Professor George. H. (G. H.) was an advanced math professor at Colorado. He sounded like a roaring lion as he taught, filling up the blackboard with sketches and equations so fast I could barely keep up. It was hopeless to take notes and concentrate on what he was saying at the same time. I had to ambush other students after class and ask, "What went on in there?" Usually they were happy to explain. G. H. invited students to his office if they needed help. I took his offer once when I was hopelessly confused and started down a long, dark hallway to his office. Sudden fear struck me when I saw what looked like his severed head, white hair, bushy eyebrows, beard, and moustache, floating in the darkness! I froze! The head spoke, "Come in!" I forgot why I came, I was so terrified! It turned out to be his reflection in a mirror on his desk so he could see if someone was approaching in the hallway. He was warm and friendly. I remembered, asked my questions, and went home. His friendliness outside the classroom impressed me. *I wanted to be friendly both inside and outside the classroom. (I would prefer to avoid all the white hair if possible and "chamber-of-horrors" environment.)*

Professor Lou L. (L. L.) taught a Stanford graduate class to engineers from industry who were working on an advanced degree. Most of us took time off from our jobs and drove to the campus. The class had high value to us because we were learning to solve problems in the energy industry, which was the field most of us worked in. *Professor L. L.* was one of the best in the Nation. One afternoon we found that a Liberal Arts class, led by their Professor, was blocking the entrance to the engineering building where our class met when we arrived. They were protesting the Viet-Nam war.

I have no argument if someone wants to express his or her approval or disapproval to what our government may choose to do, but I disagree when their reaction interferes with the freedoms the rest of us enjoy (and pay taxes for), or when they interfere with an opportunity my company is paying for. We didn't wait long. *Professor L. L.,* a husky man, came from his office in another building. He saw the line of picketing students, lowered his head like a fullback carrying his briefcase like a football player crashing the line for the winning touchdown, and plowed through, sending protestors and signs in every direction. The rest of us followed him to the classroom. He taught a useful applied course in thermodynamics (yes, it is useful!) that would ultimately make life better for others anywhere in the world. *Professor L. L. inspired me with the desire to show that my classes had long-range benefits for others by providing humanitarian applications.*

There was another occasion when over thirty graduate engineers from industry were waiting in a classroom for our first encounter with *Bill R. (B. R.),* a new Stanford professor. A boyish-looking "kid" walked in with a large binder that he laid on the front table. He studied the class a moment, and then introduced himself. I thought, "They are sending a high-school kid to teach a graduate course?" He took a piece of chalk and drew a picture of a complex energy system. Then he wrote the equations which governed its behavior. He explained that it represented a real problem he had been hired to solve for a Bay Area company. By then all of us were engaged with his lecture. He combined and simplified the equations, covered two pull-down blackboards, stuffed in numbers, erased small terms, and in 20 minutes he ended up with one short equation. "We can solve this one!" I was dumbfounded and wanted to cheer! He said, "But we don't even have to solve it. We can set this term equal to zero and there is the answer!" Silence. Then more silence. "That is what the customer is paying big bucks for!"

It wasn't the big bucks that grabbed me. It was the demonstration I had just seen. The beauty of reducing a complex problem into a simple, manageable exercise, and getting a useful solution! I wanted to learn how to do that! B. R. became my engineering mentor, and my dissertation advisor. *Most of what engineering and teaching I do today is rooted in the spirit and substance of B. R.'s fun-filled, keep-life-simple, creative, and enjoyable approach. I hope to pass that same spirit on to those in my classes.*

Those are some professors who influenced me, not only by what they taught, but by who they were in and out of the classroom.

Becoming the best teacher I can be is a goal that I always will be reaching for because no matter how good I think I might have become, or how close I might have come to being the best, I am not there. There is still distance to go—improvements to be made—gaps to close. Some goals we can set, and when we reach them we go on to another goal. When it comes to a goal like "being the best we can be," that is a goal we can only get closer to as time and effort passes. *If we reach a specific goal, we quit trying. When it comes to an activity like teaching, which has no known limits of excellence, I want to be better each day than I was the day before as long as I live.*

> **The Lord will perfect that which concerns me; Your mercy, O Lord, endures forever; Do not forsake the works of your hands. (Psalm 138:8-a)**

I thought being an adjunct professor would be like starting a new job with a team of professors who looked at teaching like I did. Later, when the opportunity opened to teach at San Jose State University, I found out that I guessed wrong. All of us are "wired" in our search for people we can admire. What do you admire most in others? What features make the best "role models" for you? Do they have to be something you already possess or something different?

CHAPTER 33

ADJUNCT—ENEMY TO ALLY

I got off to a good start with students the first semester and had rewarding interactions with them. It was not the same with the department faculty. They welcomed me politely at first although in the days that followed they were cold and shunning. The department chairmen were different—they were the *bosses* of the department faculty, and they appreciated my coming to help in the department. With an abundance of students, they had to open duplicate sessions of some classes and appealed to industry for temporary instructors to teach those classes. But most of the faculty—the teaching professors who taught identical class sessions—avoided me. It was like they thought I was competing with them rather than working on the same team! They even ignored my friendly hallway greetings.

I had not hurt anyone. I had not insulted anyone. I had not said anything unkind to any of them. But most of these professors had a low view of me. There had to be some other reason. Did I impress them as a *know-it-all* who thought he was *the grand engineer from industry* who came to save the department? Maybe I had given them the impression that I thought I was *better than they were*. I don't see how. None of us talked to each other!

One day I overheard two professors talking. "They can't afford a full-time position, but they've got money for part-time morons from industry, who think they can teach courses that they don't know anything about. These so-called *professors* only confuse students while they add another *accomplishment* to their resumé." Now I knew why the professors were upset toward me and the other part-timers! I wanted to defend myself and straighten out their thinking! But how could I convince them? It sounded like their minds were already made up. "What Should I Do Now?"

I don't recall when I heard this biblical principle, and I was not thinking of it then, but deep down it must have been whispering a way to handle the situation with the professors who despised my being there. It goes like this:

> **Let nothing be done through selfish ambition or conceit, but in lowliness of mind let each esteem others better than himself. Let each of you look out not only for his own interests, but also for the interests of others.**
> **(Philippians 2:3, 4)**

The validity of that principle was proved in the days that followed. Opportunities opened where I could speak briefly to one professor at a time. I would say something like, "You know, I am one of the 'imports from industry' to help the department with the overflow of students. I don't have any delusions—I need all the help I can get. I know you are a top-notch prof. in the department, so let me ask you something." Usually with that, I had my listener by the ear. Then I could follow up with one or two questions about his teaching methods. Most professors turned warm toward me at that point and shared their philosophy of teaching with enthusiasm! Soon, we would be talking like old friends! Either then, or later over coffee follow-ups, they would share more. After similar conversations with other suspicious professors, they began to greet me in the halls! (... *esteem others better than myself*...I admitted I was not the "know-it-all" they might have expected, and I wanted to learn from them.)

As the semester progressed, I became more of an *ally* than an *enemy* with most of the other professors. By the end of the second semester some professors were urging me to join them at their monthly lunches held in local restaurants. I had become one of the family, although some of them still gave the impression that if anyone saw them speak to me, they would be judged as if they were speaking to the devil himself!

I saw someone studying my homework solutions behind the glass frame outside the chairman's office. At first I thought he was a student comparing his answers with mine, but none of my students had grey hair. He was one of the still-suspicious professors critically examining my answers. He might have been looking for flaws to verify his suspicions about me. (I think he had to give it an *A* grade.)

Another time I posted a new solution method that was not in the textbook for a heat transfer problem I was teaching. Another full-time professor, who was teaching another section of the same course, still suspected my competence. He was busy copying the solution. I doubt that he had ever seen it, because it was new and recently published. I felt pretty smart that afternoon, realizing that I had taught something to another professor with a lot more experience than I had. (He never mentioned it, and neither did I.)

At the faculty lunches and dinners where I was invited, one or two glasses of wine resulted in amazing transformations. Some of the professors became—the kindest way to say it is—clowns. They were not the people I knew at the university! Their garbled language turned to various diatribes that were between comedy, anger, sarcasm, filth, and sadness. One professor boasted that he had flunked half of his class, as if this was worthy of merit! Another started a sequence of dirty jokes. (There were no women present.) The more wine, the looser the talk. I don't claim to be better as I only sipped ginger ale—I never learned to like wine or hard liquor. But when I saw what wine did to these living pillars of knowledge, it made me more convinced that I could never be the role model I wanted to be if I ever let wine pull back the curtain and expose that part of me that I worked hard to overcome!

Some professors had unusual preferences. The most friendly professor with the longest tenure, who also was an established resident of the Bay Area, surprised me that twice a year he made a pilgrimage to Los Angeles for a dental appointment! He liked a certain dentist and had stayed with him since childhood even though it meant a long commute. The uncertainty of what to do about a sudden toothache or broken tooth didn't seem to bother him. Compared to average costs of a trip to the dentist, I think the round-trip air fare would only be a blip.

One of the long-term professors and I found each other attending the same engineering conference in New Orleans. GE had sent me, and the university paid his expenses. The department secretary had a son-in-law, Wendell, who played first trumpet in the famous Preservation Hall Jazz Band, a highlight of New Orleans. It wasn't what we expected, sitting on old floor cushions listening to the band, who were in their 80s and 90s—except for Wendell. They took a collection to play their signature "When the Saints Go Marchin' In." By the second round, the entire audience was clapping hands and slapping their knees while they sang along! It was a rip-roarin' church service, no matter what you called yourself!

The professor and I spent many hours together that week. The third day he began to discuss things that bothered him personally and divulged some deep hurts. I could identify with his pain and a friendship based on mutual trust was forming. He was open to encouragement I offered him from my experience that I had found from biblical truths that worked for me.

Therefore humble yourselves under the mighty hand of God, that He may exalt you in due time, casting all your care upon Him for He cares for you. (I Peter 5:6, 7)

I find that academia is not much different than the everyday world where most of us live. It is stocked with people that may rank high on the worldly *knowledge, understanding, and wisdom scales*, but when you penetrate those scales and learn who these people really are, you find that they are like the rest of us. They are entirely human. They are people who are living with hopes, hurts, ambitions, aspirations, pain of many kinds, disappointments, plans, loneliness, regrets, and a need for another person who cares—a friend to share life with.

Regardless of how people hold back their innermost feelings, they usually open up to one who has earned their trust as a friend. They feel safe to share their mountain tops, as well as the broken fragments of their lives. That may open the following opportunities:

***Rejoice with those who rejoice, and weep with those who weep.* (Romans 12:15)**

***Bear one another's burdens and so fulfill the law of Christ.* (Galatians 6:2)**

> Have you ever been shunned by a group you tried belonging to? Were you able to discover why? Have you discovered ways to win over those in the group?

CHAPTER 34

LEARNING FROM STUDENTS

I parked my car in the multi-level garage across from San Jose State University. This would be my first class meeting of undergraduate students. Something grabbed my attention. "Was that what I think it was?" It looked like someone falling. I rushed to see a young man lying on the sidewalk five stories below. He had to be a student, judging from the backpack next to him with textbooks scattered out of it. By the time I hurried out of the garage a crowd had surrounded him. A woman had rushed from across the street with towels to place around his head as he vomited blood. Someone said an ambulance was on the way.

There was nothing I could do, so I went to class, although sickened. From then, I realized that college students were special human beings. Some perhaps were cutting the cord from home for the first time. This was *unchartered waters* for some, and finding the right path to fulfillment can be threatening. Still others, with no outward signs, could be very troubled and afraid, not knowing how to cope with new, sometimes unfriendly experiences. They may have hopes, dreams, emotions, feelings, and goals. But they need guidance and affirmation, and they need people who genuinely care about them whom they can trust. How do I know? I have been a student just like them! They may want to appear self-sufficient and independent, but since I have been one, I know what it can be like. Students need living models who care for them beyond the attention only given to a registration number. I aspired to be a teacher like that at every opportunity.

It was unexpected events that resulted in me climbing the stairs to the classroom that day. A week before, there was no such plan. I was walking past Bob's office at GE. He knew that I taught technical classes to the newly-hired engineers and he called to me, "How would you like to teach a class at San Jose State? They're understaffed and need someone from industry to help out. They can't pay, but we can give you the time off." I seized the opportunity. Now I was walking into a classroom of 32 young men and women. Their chattering suddenly stopped and they began to study me.

It took two minutes to sense that the class liked my approach. "If I told you I work at GE, that wouldn't be entirely accurate. It would be more accurate for me to say that I have a lot of fun at GE solving problems in fluid mechanics to pay the bills. In my view, being an engineer can be one of the most fun-filled jobs that exists. My job here is to show you how you can have that kind of fun, too. Everyone likes to have fun, and your job should be like that. If it's not, then you're in the wrong profession. So let's jump in and have some fun with the problems in Chapter 1."

I had learned that one of the secrets of keeping the attention of a class is to drop stories or surprises into the lectures. "You've heard the legend about the little boy who kept Holland from being flooded by plugging a leak in the dike with his finger? Did you know that if he had pulled his finger out to scratch his butt, the jet of water coming through the leak would have had such force that he would not have been able to put his finger back into the leak? We're going to prove that today—and we won't have to go to Holland!"

Another time it was homecoming weekend and the focus of students on Friday afternoon classes was everywhere but in the classroom. I chose one of the most intriguing technical examples found in the literature and drew it on the blackboard. The class quieted down when I asked a simple question. It was obvious they suspected me. Then I added something to the sketch and showed the surprising result. A tiny bubble in a sealed tank filled with liquid, rising from the bottom to the top, doubles the tank pressure. For a moment I thought I was deaf. No one said a word—no one moved a pencil—there was not a whisper. Then suddenly Omar, a student from Egypt sitting in the front, slammed his hand on the desk! "No!" he yelled, jolting the entire class. "It isn't so! You can't get something for nothing! You're violating some law! I don't believe it!"

By that time, everyone was animated and watching. "Omar," I said quietly, "I just proved it is true! No laws are broken! It is all in front of you! It is just an unexpected result!"

We argued for five minutes, but he did not hear a word I said. All he could say was that he did not believe the result. It could not be true. I could not convince him. The bell rang. But Omar did not give up. He went to his advisor, who agreed with him, that what I had said was bogus! Then Omar went to the head of the physics department who also sympathized. Omar was reinforced and had determined to take his case to the ombudsman on Monday, but never did because the physicist built a small model to check the absurd result—and he found that it was true! So, Omar cooled off and had to accept truth instead of his *gut feel*. The class loved it. Omar graduated and later became an engineer for General Electric.

One of the strangest requests came from a student who played by his own rules. Even though the class was designed to be useful and fun, there was the matter of grades. Three quizzes and a final exam would determine the final letter grade. One student did not attend class or take any of the quizzes. He came for the final exam and wrote his name on it. I wrote an "Incomplete" for him on the university grade sheet, because I thought he must have had family problems to keep him away from class. At least an "Inc." would give him a chance to retake the class at another time and he would not lose tuition money. I guessed wrong.

He called my phone number and said he needed an A so he could graduate. He was serious. Apparently he needed an additional five-unit course to graduate and put down my course, thinking it would be a formality to give him an A for graduation. No amount of reasoning helped. It was worse than trying to convince Omar! If I didn't give him an A, I would be the one person who prevented him from graduating! "Now, just a minute. All the other students worked hard for their grades. Very hard. You didn't lift a finger and say I should give you an A? You think that is fair? You really should have an F, and I was trying to help you with an 'Incomplete' grade." The conversation ended with an angry student slamming the receiver.

The first school year passed and San Jose asked me to remain on their adjunct list. They kept me active teaching one or two courses each semester for 17 years, making student friends and following the progress of many.

I told students that my last class of each semester was optional because I wouldn't be talking about fluid mechanics. Instead, I would tell them some basic principles I had learned for living life with purpose and meaning. It would be my personal story that might give them some ideas to add to their own lives. Whether they came to the class or not would have no effect on their grade. Almost everyone came. They received an outline of my talk entitled, *The Seven Laws of Success*, which is summarized in the Appendix of this book. It describes personal examples and biblical truths that are open to all who believe.

Some of the most treasured results from my adjunct years are the notes and other communications students took time to send. A few samples are listed next:

> *Prof. Moody: I had problems in your class. My 1st midterm score was 38/100, but you encouraged me to work harder. I improved my second midterm score to 71/100, and then 96/100 on the third. Thank you for teaching me fluid mechanics, but more importantly, that with hard work I can achieve success. Thank you for your inspiration and caring. I enjoyed your stories. Yours truly, S. V.*
>
> *FROM A DYSLEXIC STUDENT: Dear Dr. Moody: When I enrolled in ME 111, I was very nervous about the material. This was because I didn't know I was going to have such a good*

instructor. You were able to simplify everything so that we, as students, could understand. I also wanted to express my thanks to you for being understanding of my testing situation. Your student, G. L.

Dear Professor Moody: I just wanted to take the time to thank you and tell you how much I appreciated your kindness and your humor throughout the semester. So many people seem to teach because of the power; you obviously teach because you like to. That is very refreshing. You went out of your way for us—both to keep the class when it was threatened, and to make yourself available to your students. You're a special person and you deserve to be reminded of it. Sincerely, R. B.

Dear Mr. Moody: I'm writing to you regarding your speech you gave on the last day of class. You really opened my eyes to a new way of looking at God and the Bible. Your timing was perfect as well. I was really stressed out about school, my boyfriend dumped me, and I was overall just feeling lousy about myself. I turned to my friends and my mother for support, but I still felt that something was lacking. When you talked about the time in your life where you felt like you were going nowhere and how you turned things around by looking to God, it made me think about if God could have that kind of positive impact on my life as well. I plan on reading the Bible again. I think that "The Seven Laws of Success" that you outlined in class will help me just as it helped you in your career. I just want to say thank you, Mr. Moody. You've been an inspiration to me. You've been an excellent instructor and a role model for many people. Sincerely, M. F.

Dear Dr. Moody: I attended your optional "God wants me to build nuclear power plants," lecture at the end of the semester. I went away puzzled that a great scientist would give credit for his intellect to God, when it obviously came from himself. My previous understanding of God came from my father, and was when you're bad you got sent to church, and if you want something you pray for it. Well, I never got what I prayed for, which mostly was to have my dad stop being verbally abusive to me. So I gave up on the idea of God. Later, as a student of science, it was obvious that since you couldn't scientifically prove He existed, He didn't. I got into the habit of not believing. But after hearing you talk, I thought about it a lot, and decided several things—that some things you can take on faith; I'm an adult and I'm not afraid if my friends laugh at me; and I might as well go to church and see if I get anything out of it. It turned out that my old church (Greek Orthodox Annunciation in SF) had a new priest, unprejudiced and open-minded, and more of the service in English, so now I sing in the choir and go regularly (every 2 weeks). I can't make it to our Bible study, but I try to read and pray on my own. I think you were one of the main reasons I became not embarrassed to think about God, and why I am moving toward becoming more complete. I wanted you to know that you gave me more than an education in fluid mechanics, something that will be more valuable in the long run. A. M.

Other professors receive letters of appreciation citing the personal care and interest they have shown to students. The samples above show how some students evaluate what they perceived in one who stood in front of them teaching something—often more than what was in the book.

The heart of the prudent acquires knowledge, and the ear of the wise seeks knowledge. (Proverbs 18: 15)

Instruct the wise, and they will be even wiser. Teach the righteous, and they will learn even more. (Proverbs 9: 9)

Whenever we give knowledge to another person and help them understand how to use it, we're teaching. Can you think of someone who would call you a teacher? Also, you are a learner when someone is teaching you. Would you rather teach or learn? Are there times when you think, "This person can't tell me anything I don't already know." What would you say to that?

CHAPTER 35

GALLBLADDER

My wife, Phyllis woke up with a pain in the middle of her stomach one Friday. The usual antacids and painkillers did not help and by noon she wanted me to drive her to her doctor. Whenever she wanted to see her doctor, I knew it was serious because she had a high tolerance for pain. Phyllis had diagnosed herself: *Diverticulitis—a* problem where small cavities in your large intestine get infected. Her mom had suffered from it and it can be inherited. She held her head with one hand with eyes closed while I drove.

The doctor pressed lightly until she found the spot where Phyllis almost screamed. "That's too high to be diverticulitis-- it must be your gallbladder instead." The doctor gave her a shot for pain and told us to contact a surgeon in San Andreas ASAP. "He's the best. He may want to remove it." The pain was easing when we left the office.

"The soonest I can give you an appointment is three months," was the answer I got when I called the office of the *best* surgeon. Even when I explained that Phyllis's doctor said this needed quick action, it was ignored. "I'm sorry, that's the best I can do." I hung up before calling her a liar. My blood pressure was pushing my eyeballs out of their sockets.

Counting to ten was not enough. "What Should I Do Now?"

I looked up other surgeons and found several with Middle Eastern and South African names. With a wife who would be in pain again when the shot wore off, it didn't matter what their names were, or how many shrunken heads dangled from their uniforms! I called one office and they cheerfully made an appointment for Monday.

WHAT SHOULD I DO NOW?

We were watching TV Friday evening and Phyllis began to moan. The pain had returned, more intense than before. I said, "I'm going to take you to San Andreas ER to get you another shot for pain. Maybe they will give you some pain pills to get you through Sunday." It was a painful drive to the hospital, and an agonizing 20 minutes in the waiting room before they took her in for paperwork and checking. Several tests must have told the story because as we waited in an empty room, the ER doctor came in. He was a big, muscular Afro-American, built like a San Francisco Forty-Niners linebacker. "You got a gallbladder problem, ma'am!" Phyllis agreed. "I think it's in bad shape, too! We don't want to send you home with that, do we?" She shook her head. "Will it be OK if we take it out?" This was not a time for a family council, or detailed discussion with relatives and friends. We did not need anyone else's advice, or personal opinion, or horror story. Both of us enthusiastically agreed. "Take it out! Now! Please!"

Within a few minutes she was prepped for surgery while I signed papers. "By the way," said the ER doctor, "The surgeon on call is Dr. So and So." I don't remember his name now, but he was the *best surgeon* referred to by Phyllis's doctor, whose front office Command Post told us we couldn't see him for three months! I met him after the surgery when he gave me instructions for Phyllis's care when she came home. "It was good timing," he said. "Three small holes, but a very sick gallbladder! Partly gangrene!" He gave me color photos of Phyllis's insides where he did the surgery. There was no reason for the surgeon to see her again unless there were problems. Her regular doctor could take care of most questions.

Phyllis's doctor told us that according to the surgeon's report, if we had waited one or two more days, it could have been life-threatening. The surgeon proved his skill by doing a remarkable surgery, and Phyllis made a fast recovery. But some obstacles still are beyond any amount of surgical or other human skill. In this case, it took a big, muscular, caring ER doctor plus a miracle from heaven to do an *end run* around the surgeon's front office.

We were able to cancel our Monday appointment with an unknown doctor, but we thanked his office for being able to fit us in so promptly.

"For My thoughts are not your thoughts, nor are your ways My ways," says the Lord. "For as the heavens are higher than the earth, so are My ways higher than your ways, and My thoughts than your thoughts." (Isaiah 55:8,9)

Do you remember a time when you felt warmed by God's presence and the assurance that He had arranged events, people, and places in a way that showed He was caring for you? Others will be encouraged to hear you tell about it, especially if they are facing a similar circumstance.

CHAPTER 36

UNREALIZED GIFT

(This chapter is based on a speech I gave at the District 33 Annual Toastmasters International Conference, April 25-27, 2024 at Oxnard, CA. It came under the "Humorous Speech" category and won First Place. The narrative describes true events, reported from vivid memory recall.)

I joined the old-timers hurrying toward the Murphys Town Hall for our monthly *Sons In Retirement (SIRS)* meeting. SIRS is a National Knife and Fork Club for men between retirement and the last rites who meet for lunch and a speaker every month. The attendance was double today because the speaker was a Forty-Niners cheerleader! All I knew about the 49ers cheerleaders came from a calendar in a mini-market: Heavy lipstick, flowing hair, long eyelashes, polished fingernails, wide smiles, white teeth, and skimpy outfits with enough skin showing for a mosquito paradise.

Someone asked one old guy with an oxygen tank, being pushed in a wheelchair if this might be too risky for him. He replied, "I may be on my deathbed, but I still got a pulse!" Other men had dug out their 60-year old fancy duds that smelled like mothballs, and some wore white bucks. A few had polo shirts partly open to expose wiry chest hairs. Their eyeglasses sparkled like they had been through a carwash. Some still with hair had new haircuts, trimmed beards that were reeking of aftershave, and looking like they were going on a hot date.

The town hall sounded like half-time at a game. "Hurry up! Keep the line moving!" New arrivals were straining to find Ms. Cheerleader. "There she is!" She was at the far end, corralled by a group of men who were engaged in lively conversations with her. She was dressed conservatively in a long-sleeved white blouse, a modest pant suit, and any young man would be proud to introduce her to his old-fashioned parents. But that isn't what was on display.

This young woman had a gift! She was igniting the souls of some old guys I had never seen smile or laugh before! Some of those men were always scowling like they had been weaned on a dill pickle, but today they were laughing! She drew life out of them! They enjoyed responding to her happy, uplifting reactions to their questions and comments. Some of the men were still married. I asked the SIRS president if their wives might object. "Naw, they look at it like a dog chasing after cars. If he ever caught one, he wouldn't know what to do with it."

"Take your seats! Time for lunch." I doubt if anyone remembers what was served. The piano player let go with the 49er theme song. There was a prayer and the Pledge of Allegiance. Ms. Cheerleader sat between the SIRS President and vice president, who each had their heads turned 90 degrees to eat and carry on a conversation with her. Probably both went to the chiropractor the next day. Then she spoke. Cheerleaders got paid $35 per game, but a lot more for endorsements, and free travel and hotels, so they did well financially. She also had a photography business—child and family portraits, and glamour pictures of aspiring models. She had made the Playboy centerfold, and that's when she decided on a career in modeling.

Time for questions and answers. I thought now we would learn what a cheerleader's life really was like. A hand shot up. "What kind of camera do you use?" Another hand—"What kind of film?" I thought, "What a waste with useless questions! Who cares about her camera? So I raised my hand.

"I have teenage granddaughters. What advice would you have for them?" The room got deathly quiet—and so did Ms. Cheerleader. She cleared her throat while thinking about an answer. "Well, if they're pretty—if they have nice figures, they could be models." She went on about modeling school, finding opportunities, and getting lots of public exposure. Her response was painful for her and the audience. Another hand went up. "Do you ever shoot landscapes?"

The meeting was over. We had blown a once-in-a-lifetime opportunity for a personal interview with a beautiful young woman who took time to be with men old enough to be her grandfather, and make them laugh and smile. She had a gift she probably didn't know she had. I hope she realizes what a powerful hidden talent she possesses long before the Botox fails and the skin begins to sag and wrinkles are hard to hide. How she can lift older people out of their humdrum existences, making them smile and laugh and engage with her; how she showed that she could communicate with them from her heart. There will always be a place for a person like Ms. Cheerleader—not on calendars, but cheering and inspiring the older and sometimes forgotten folks, helping them realize they have more life to live.

...the Lord does not see as man sees; for man looks at the outward appearance, but the Lord looks at the heart.
(I Samuel 16:7b)

> It is possible that we also have "hidden talents." We may not have discovered them yet, but when we do, they might be applied in remarkable ways. Young people need affirmation and motivation; older people need contact and encouragement; others just need someone to come alongside and be there for them. Does that describe one of your talents that may not be hidden after all?

CHAPTER 37

DREAM ROBBERS

My middle school science teacher horrified our class when he described a biological experiment. The boys sat like stone statues at full attention. The girls shuddered. "If you take a frog," he said, "and drop him into hot water, he will jump out. But if you put him into a pot of cool water and heat the water slowly, the frog will stay in the water* and be boiled to death." That meant we could have frog legs for dinner, and if we were very hungry, we could eat the whole frog! The boys broke into a cheer and asked where we could get a frog! Some kid asked how you could be sure it was a boy frog? The teacher had told an age-old story that has been repeated by politicians and speakers to warn us that we are like frogs. We resist sudden changes. If we fall into hot water, we jump out. However, we tolerate gradual physical, economic, and political changes that could ruin our lives, like being slowly boiled to death.

*derivate_The New Psychology_ (1897): 19th-century experiments were purported to show that frogs did not attempt to escape gradually heated water. An 1872 experiment by Heinzmann was said to show that a normal frog would not attempt to escape if the water was heated slowly enough, which was corroborated in 1875 by Fratscher. Heinzmann heated the frogs over the course of 90 minutes from about 21 °C (70 °F) to 37.5 °C (99.5 °F), a rate of less than 0.2 °C (0,36 /F°) per minute. (Continued heating would have likely resulted in a dead lab specimen.)

I've been robbed!

Sometimes we know right away that we have been robbed. The door lock is broken, the apartment is torn up, and valuables are missing. We know right away what happened, like being dropped into hot water. Ouch! We don't think—we react! Jump out! Dial the police!

My oldest son, a retired police sergeant still active on the reserves, left home to drive his suburban to work. The vehicle was gone! The parking space was empty! His outside security tapes showed two men at 2:00 AM break the lock and drive it away in less than a minute. He forgot to set the alarm. It was a routine robbery where thieves steal and hide a vehicle in a garage, dismantle it, take the parts they can sell, and abandon the body on a lonely road. His vehicle was found with parts missing. That familiar scenario happens every night in cities big and small. He knew immediately he had been robbed, like he would have known if he was dropped into a tub of boiling water.

There are times when someone thinks they can avoid being dropped into hot water if they act quickly. Like one grandmother we know who got a frantic phone message. The caller, claiming to be a friend of her grandson, told her a crime had occurred and her grandson was falsely accused. He'd be held in jail in a distant city unless he paid a legal fee of $10,000.00 *immediately*. The grandson thought his grandmother could wire the money to keep him out of jail. The grandmother panicked and paid the *legal fee* to a phony law firm from her retirement savings. If she had dialed her grandson's cell phone, he would have affirmed that he and his family were all OK. *Robbed!* She jumped out of the hot water but in a panic, she reacted in the worst way. That same scheme has robbed many people of millions.

Stopping a robbery by speaking up

A young man from my Toastmasters club was in a grocery checkout line behind a biker. Ahead of the biker was an elderly woman, paying for her groceries while fumbling for bills from her purse. She did not see a $10 bill drop to the floor. The biker put his boot on the bill hiding it as the woman continued to hand money to the clerk. The Toastmaster called to the woman in a voice that the clerk and others nearby could hear, "Ma'am! You dropped a ten-dollar bill on the floor—and this nice gentleman put his foot on it to keep it from blowing away." The biker glared at him and gave the bill to the woman, who thanked him. The biker was waiting for the Toastmaster outside the store, where he threatened him and called him dirty names before roaring off on his motorcycle. *Almost* a robbery! This time pain and loss were avoided,-- at least for the woman! Sadly, you can generate hate and anger for an act of kindness. "What Should I Do Now?" Of course the answer is, "Do the right thing even if it costs something."

Credit cards can be the unlocked safe

Whenever something of mine is stolen, I react. Sometimes I get angry, but I don't know where to direct the anger. It saps energy to get angry, and the best way I found to avoid the wear-and-tear of anger is to bring it to God and ask Him to intervene—as if He doesn't have bigger things to work on. But He actually wants us to do that. Consider His words,

… do not avenge yourselves, but rather give place to wrath, for it is written, "Vengeance is Mine, I will repay," says the Lord. **(Romans 12:19)**

Sometimes I just feel sorrowful—other times like a victim with no one to help. Once my credit card information was stolen when a dishonest clerk passed it on to a gang that made some large overseas purchases with it before the bank notified me of unusual activity. They cancelled the card without holding me responsible for purchases that were not mine (bless them!) It took several months to smooth out various accounts so creditors wouldn't charge late fees when they couldn't collect from the cancelled card.

If small value items are stolen, like a favorite pen, my reaction is a notched-down irritation. Everything will rot, decay, melt, or wear out someday—so why should their absence cause me to suffer? Jesus said,

Do not lay up for yourselves treasures on earth, where moth and rust destroy and where thieves break in and steal; but lay up for

yourselves treasures in heaven, where neither moth nor rust destroys and where thieves do not break in and steal. For where your treasure is, there your heart will be also.
(Matthew 6:19-21)

One application of that advice might be: *If you have a dream, don't leave it out where it can be stolen, but rather make the effort to protect it*

An old parable describes a wealthy man with so much produce and goods that he ran out of space to keep it. He decided to build huge, new bins and fill them with his possessions; then he could say, "You have much stored up! Eat, drink, and be merry!"

But God said to him, "Fool! This night your soul will be required of you; then whose will those things be which you have provided?" So is he who lays up treasure for himself, and is not rich toward God.
(Luke 12:20, 21)

There is a *life principle* here for anyone regardless of their personal faith. It involves the *dreams* we may have for the future. Sadly, just as we can be robbed of possessions, we can be robbed of our dreams.

What happened to my dream?

It was my seventh year as an engineer with the GE Nuclear Energy Department and Phyllis and I had rented a house with a huge back yard for our first two sons to romp in.

This personal dream of a happy family was coming true. I had given our checkbook to Phyllis so she could be the family bookkeeper. She paid the bills and made sure our checking account stayed above zero. She used to go about the house humming happy songs, but that slowly stopped. She showed me that with our first son enrolled in a Christian school kindergarten, the tuition was sucking up every cent. She blamed herself for poor budgeting and was unhappy most of the time. *My happy family dream* was fading!

My solution? She should check with her friends on better ways to budget. But things only got worse and she was unhappy most of the time. We finally saw a counselor who told me that being a *family bookkeeper* was not Phyllis's talent, and I should relieve her of that responsibility. I could handle the check-writing, shielding her from blame if we came up short. Amazingly, Phyllis began humming tunes and was happy again. My happy family dream was restored. She would scratch my back while I was scratching my head writing checks. I faced the same problems she had faced. I couldn't make the credit card debt decrease! "What Should I Do Now?" But we did hold our debt from getting out of sight and Phyllis was happy again.

Obstacles VS a dream

My youngest son, Dan, had dreamed of becoming a police officer from the time he began to watch *Adam 12*, a police television program. He wanted "to catch the bad guys so he could make people safe." He played cops and robbers with his friends, and got to know policemen as he grew up. After several years of college, he reached a point where he could apply to a department, hoping to be hired and sent to the police academy. That was the normal route to becoming a policeman—you get hired by a department, they send you to the academy for training at their expense, then you become a member of that department. But he could not find a department with an opening. After rejections because of no open positions at dozens of departments in and out of California, he gave up and settled for a job as foreman at a California landfill. He was almost robbed of his dream by a steady stream of rejections.

Dan's dream of being a cop would have died except for his older brother encouraging him to pay his own way through the police academy, and then apply at a police department. He did this and was hired by the town of Los Gatos. He was almost robbed of his lifelong dream by circumstances beyond his control, but brotherly encouragement was all he needed to push on the door one more time. It opened and his dream became a reality. (We believe that the prayers of Mom and Dad, friends and family helped him to keep pushing.) Now he is a homicide detective working his dream job of catching killers and making a safer environment for the people of southeastern California.

It ain't over 'til it's over

American baseball legend Yogi Berra first said this phrase about baseball›s 1973 National League pennant race. His team was behind and they rallied to win the division title.

After my wife died, a close friend said, "Fred, you have to have something that gets you up in the morning besides a busting bladder!" He meant some activity that I enjoyed too much to stay in bed. I was fortunate to be connected to Toastmasters clubs and several weekly coffee breaks with friends, so I didn't have to look far for *those things* that got me up.

I know others who haven't found *those things* that make them jump out of bed, anticipating another day to do something enjoyable. They are in *death's waiting room* and need to be coaxed or dragged to the *playground* where they will discover that God did not put them out to pasture. Instead, He has a new, rewarding life plan for them.

If I were one of those people—retired with no pressing responsibilities, and someone dropped me as a newcomer into the *playground*, I would ask, "Where is that new, rewarding plan I am supposed to find here?" Looking around, here's what I might see:

* Several retired men who began cutting and splitting fallen trees in Big Trees State Park, delivering cords of firewood to poor families that depended on wood to heat their homes. The group calls themselves the *Do-Wooders*

* One woman who started a *quilt club* in her apartment, teaching other women how to make quilts.

* A retired couple who started a book club where members meet weekly to discuss a book they were reading.

* One retired man who started a photo club and leads groups on photo tours while showing how to take creative pictures, some of which have won prizes.

* A group of retired women who started a craft club that makes novelty gift items which they take on visits to shut-in neighbors and friends.

* Several couples who established a game night for retired friends each week.

* Others have a movie night each week with dinner at a local restaurant followed by a movie at a theater.

* Quite a few who play weekly chess games, bridge, or rounds of pool.

* Some simply gather on a regular basis to enjoy a cup of cider, coffee, or hot chocolate by one of the parlor fireplaces and reminisce.

* One couple volunteered at a museum as Docents

* Some people volunteer to help at the gospel mission. One man teaches English.

* The list keeps growing…..

Everywhere I look, I see those who are living the new, rewarding plan God designed for them when they may have thought they were useless. It can no longer be said of them,

How long will you slumber, O sluggard? When will you rise from your sleep? A little sleep, a little slumber, a little folding of the hands

to sleep—so shall your poverty come on you like a prowler, and your need like an armed man. **(Proverbs 6: 9-11)**

For I know the thoughts that I think toward you, says the Lord, thoughts of peace and not of evil, to give you a future and a hope. **(Jeremiah 29: 11)**

> Most of us dream about what our lives will be like in the future: where we will be living; what we will be doing; which people will be our friends, associates, and neighbors; will we be happy? Our dreams usually are positive because of the way most of us are made. Life is fragile, and just like objects that can be stolen, our dreams are vulnerable to robbery. How would you advise someone to protect their dreams?

CHAPTER 38

SELF-ROBBERY

A friend of mine climbed to the high-dive, even though he had never dived into a pool. He walked to the end of the board 30 feet above the water, showing no fear. Then he took a deep breath and jumped. I gasped as he tucked into a tight ball and hit the surface with a huge splash. I was afraid he might kill himself, but my fear disappeared when he popped up to the surface laughing. I wouldn't have done that at gunpoint! Fear would have stopped me.

Another time I was with a team of engineers in former Yugoslavia. We were on a beach by the Adriatic Sea looking at a small island a quarter of a mile away. One of the team asked if anyone wanted to swim with him to the island for exercise. No one knew anything about that huge body of water, its currents, tides, marine life, or wave action, so no one accepted his invitation. He had to be joking—a crazy idea with no boats on the water, no lifeguards, and no way to help if he needed to be rescued. Several started to laugh, but stopped when they saw he was already swimming. It was an hour before we saw him stand up on the island and wave at us. Then he disappeared for another hour until he crawled back onto the beach triumphantly. Brave? Confident? Or stupid? I won't judge.

I have a built-in *fear meter* that sounds an alarm and warns me not to take risks like he took. My level of fear wouldn't let me swim one stroke toward that island. But there are times when my *fear meter* warns me not to take a risk that maybe I should take because… …If I don't take some risks I will not make progress.

It bothers me to admit that everything we do comes with a risk—a risk of harm, injury, illness, failure, damage, embarrassment, disappointment, loss, death, or other unpleasant result. Climbing stairs, crossing the street, driving, riding a bus, a plane, an elevator, going to the mall, taking a vacation, answering the phone, submitting an application, an exam, or almost any activity you can name has a risk factor. Something can always go wrong! Something can fail! Malfunction! Break! Collapse! Wear out! Something we don't expect can damage a good plan.

It should be safer to stay inside our *comfort zone* and never risk anything by going outside. (Some people do that. They are known as hermits, or recluses, anti-socials, unfriendly agoraphobics, and even people haters.) All is supposed to be peace and quiet inside one's comfort zone. Why leave the confines of our protected space (unless we can't find the remote)? But even that space can be bombed, gassed, burned or otherwise destroyed! If we leave our comfort zone, we risk something. Even if we stay inside, we are at risk. But it has been like that forever. Some are paralyzed by the thought that if they make the wrong move, they might never be heard from again.

We can't always choose the risks we have to take to make progress toward a goal. For example, we find that swimming is the only way to cross the final stream separating us from our goal. The stream is wide, deep, and home to alligators. In order to progress to our goal, we have to take that risk and either swim across, tie some logs together to make a raft, or give up reaching our goal. "What Should I Do Now?"

It's no use waiting for a voice from somewhere or a message to be written in the sand saying what to do. My *fear meter* sounded the alarm. It's up to me to decide if the goal is worth taking the risk, and then what I should do.

I knew I would be taking a risk when I enrolled in a class that would be difficult because it would require a lot of time. I avoided it as long as I could. When I finally tried to enroll, it was full. (I was glad.) I had to wait until it was offered again. That was OK with me--it gave me time to analyze why I didn't want to take risks. I think a trained psychologist might tell me that. Whether I take a risk is determined by the fight between my logic and emotions. Emotions may pull me in one direction—logic in the other.

Emotions

The emotion part of the fight is easy to identify—I don't like to risk because I'm afraid. Fear can dominate me. It makes me uncomfortable, alarmed, inwardly distressed and self-protective. That spills over into the logical part where the matter usually is clear in spite of emotions.

Logic

If my reasons for fear are shown to be trivial, then I can take a given risk without worry, knowing that the risk will contribute to progress toward my goal. However, there are three fears I need to confront because if I don't, they can stop me cold from taking any risk. These are the fear of: :

1. Personal Failure
2. What I must Sacrifice
3. Losing Personal Security

These *reasons for fear* may sound trivial, but they can stop me from progressing toward personal goals like a thick concrete roadblock. However, I think each reason can be destroyed/overcome with modest understanding and wisdom. I had to consider all three.

1. Personal Failure

Most people I know don't like to fail at anything. I'm afraid of anything that could cause me to fail. If something comes to me that calls for some action or decision where there is a high probability of failing, I try to avoid it. I think most of us will tackle something if the prize is big enough and we think the odds of winning are better than the odds of failing. However, the possibility of failure can be paralyzing. If we fail, our dream of reaching a goal is shattered. If we succeed, we imagine ourselves celebrating. It becomes a *live or die* event looming in front of us. I ask "What should I do now?"

We can also ask: What happens if we fail? Will the earth lurch out of orbit? Will life be over? Would we be spared a greater heartache by failing to reach the goal we hoped for? Could we miss the plane that crashed? The boat that sank? The girl or boyfriend who secretly was a criminal? What are other possible paths we can follow? Is there any path that does not have a risk of failure? Can we ensure success without failure? A life principle from Solomon gives a clue:

If the ax is dull, and one does not sharpen the edge, then he must use more strength; but <u>wisdom brings success</u>. (Ecclesiastes 10:10)

As a former boy scout, I have used a dull ax to cut down a small tree. It took me longer than another scout who had a sharp ax. I was exhausted when the tree finally fell. He was ready to cut down another. Depending on my limited strength, I was failing—failing to reach top performance. Wisdom says, "Sharpen the ax." Then I will succeed and not fail. In short, the principle says that *Wisdom brings success without fear of failure*. Where can we get wisdom? Wise people will say, **You get wisdom by confronting failure.**

My advisor urged me to extend a graduate project into a Ph.D. dissertation. But along with that, I would have to pass five qualifying oral exams. Two professors grill you at each one for a half hour to see how well you know the subjects. They don't ask "softball" questions, and most candidates spend weeks studying and worrying about these exams. Usually half of them pass. I was afraid that I might fail. If I did not pass, I would bear the title "failure" the rest of my life, at least in my view. But that was the *emotion* part. The *logic* part said If I did not take the *risk*, I would be a failure for having a once-in-a-lifetime opportunity drop at my feet that I wasted. I reasoned that It would be better to try and fail than to refuse to try at all.

When the day came, I did fail two out of five exams, but I didn't die! The earth kept rotating. I still had my family, my friends, my job—and an opportunity to retake both exams four months later. It was *do or die* the second time. I got three grey-haired spiritual women at church to pray for me—weeks before and during the exams. I thought I did worse the second time, but their prayers worked. My professor called to say I passed and I should celebrate with a martini. My grey-haired ladies and I celebrated with fruit juice.

2. What I Must Sacrifice

This was another fear I had for not taking a risk—what I might have to sacrifice. There were times I was making progress toward a goal, thrilled that every step made the pieces fit together while I anxiously anticipated completion. This enjoyable exercise consumed my full attention. I didn't want anything to stop the progress and take me away from that. Please! No interruptions, invitations, or even friendly visits when I was so close to the summit of reaching the goal. *Caution*! There is a life principle that warns against this state-of-mind:

Don't push your way to the front: don't sweet-talk your way to the top. <u>Put yourself aside</u>, and help others get ahead. Don't be obsessed with getting your own advantage. Forget yourselves long enough to lend a helping hand. (Philippians 2:3, The Message.)

Put yourself aside, and help others get ahead. That is the exact opposite of what I want to do. Doing what I don't want to do on behalf of someone else means *sacrifice*. Is any personal effort that promotes my project more important than acknowledging the value of someone else's project? A more fulfilling activity is to show someone else that I believe they have value and purpose. I may need to sacrifice my personal plans and spend time with them for that reason. My projects will survive my absence while I invest time in someone else's life. There were those who did that for me.

Several months passed while I was making rapid progress on my Stanford dissertation, working every spare hour on example cases to include. After dinner with the family, I would disappear to my desk in the bedroom and stay welded to it until long after bed time so I could take a weekly progress to my professor for review. Some evenings, my youngest son came to the doorway and saw me bent over the desk. That didn't stop him. "Dad, can we play catch?" Something inside me released acid. That was the last thing I wanted to do! But another part of me said, "Do it!" We played catch in the front yard as he practiced pitches for a half hour. Now he is grown with his own family. He told me recently, "I don't care how busy you were; you were never too busy to play catch!" I would have worked all night until I collapsed just to hear him say those words.

3. Losing Personal Security

This last fear was a big reason for me to avoid taking a risk. We feel secure when we are not threatened by anything. I think I speak for most people when I confess that *I don't like something that threatens my security*, whether it is an illness, physical harm, emotional distress, forces that limit my freedom or *anything that threatens the people I love and care for.*

Phyllis and I moved to the Mother Lode town of Murphys, California when I retired. We enjoyed pine trees, blue sky, pure air, streams, daffodils, deer, noisy woodpeckers (unfortunately a protected species) and pleasant weather. But the fall brought forest fire alerts and the possibility of evacuation, and even the loss of homes. Our security was threatened every year. Our street would be lined with fire trucks and water tank trucks, parked but ready for action if necessary. Many small children got to touch the fire trucks and have memorable conversations with these heroic first responders.

There is a huge market for *personal security*. Newspapers, magazines, periodicals, mail items, phone solicitors, TV, radio, and internet articles offer security of every kind. They call it *insurance*.

Life insurance; medical insurance; dental insurance; fire, flood, earthquake, tornado, home insurance, auto insurance, and insurance for jewelry, pets, travel—almost anything. You can purchase an insurance policy for it and feel the security of its protection. *Natural fear and wanting security can make one vulnerable to insurance salesmen.*

A financial agent helped Phyllis and me transfer our modest company savings into an IRA when we retired to Murphys. He was helpful to retirees, showing us how to minimize taxes and make good investments. Then the *greed bug* bit him. He went to a seminar sponsored by his primary company as they launched a new insurance policy which would pay significant benefits if we required long-term hospitalization. The premium also was significant.

He invited us to his office for a private discussion about this new policy while he sat behind a mahogany desk with a multi-colored flipchart beside him. Phyllis and I were his audience on the opposite side of the desk. We listened to his rehearsed sales pitch, urging us to purchase the new policy, one for each of us. My main question was, "How could we afford it?" He already had the answer. We could draw premiums from our IRA, which he had already set up for us. I did mental arithmetic that showed our IRA would be gone in 10 years. That didn't bother him. Our new policies would build up cash value by then. It was such a good deal--so valuable that nothing should stop us from purchasing them. He wanted us to have these policies so badly he had sent a nurse to our residence for a hurry-up medical approval. Then he sent his business partner (30 miles) to us to collect the first premium checks which he would hold until we signed.

Was this another case where I was afraid of taking a risk? His talk was based on *emotion*, appealing to *fear* and the terrible consequences we would face with no money to pay bills without the policy. We would lose our savings, our home, our belongings—we would have nothing! But we would have *happiness* if we had the policies with nothing to worry about.

I could see what he was trying to do. Stir our *emotions* so out of *fear*, we would buy his expensive policies. I began to think of the *logic* behind what he was saying. First, I did not like his tone. Too pushy. I felt relatively secure with our IRA, but his policies were an unknown commodity with only his enthusiastic urging. I didn't want this to be one of those "opportunities of a lifetime" that my *fear* of losing personal security would cause us to miss out. I told him I needed time to think about it. Phyllis agreed. Then he cooked his goose in front of us! He recited the scripted sales pitch *clinch***er**: "Do you mean, Mr. Moody, that you don't care enough for Phyllis to purchase this valuable protection?"

You could cut the air with a chainsaw. He looked at me. He expected me to avoid embarrassment and say, "I'll buy it," so I would assure Phyllis I cared for her. If I refused, I would be admitting I didn't care for her, and the agent would have his revenge for damage imposed on me, who would thereafter be branded "a terrible husband."

It was a cheap sales trick, and I could have knocked his front teeth down his throat at that point, but I controlled myself. I also fought to keep my forbidden vocabulary silent. I said nothing. Without words, Phyllis and I exchanged glances which we could read as, "Let's get out of here now—this should end our relationship with this greedy b _ _ _ _ _ d." We left his office, never to have more contact with him. Later another reputable financial planner said the long-term care policy was a good deal—especially for the agent and his company, but not for us. We would have provided income for them while losing our IRA.

Commit your works to the Lord, and your thoughts will be established. (Proverbs 16:3)

The simple believes every word, but the prudent considers well his steps. (Proverbs 14:15)

There have been too many times when I have acted on the enthusiastic urging of someone who was selling or promoting a product or a person. Their excitement and confidence was overwhelming, even though I did not know anything about the product or person they were highlighting. Rather than use their single endorsement, a larger sample of reactions from others would have provided useful viewpoints with different angles to give a more complete profile, more knowledge, increased understanding, and wisdom. Besides, Solomon wrote

>   ....*in the multitude of counsellors there is safety.*
> *(Proverbs 11:14 b)*

> Some amount of risk is necessary in order to make progress toward a goal. Do you have a method for deciding if a risk is worth taking?

CHAPTER 39

TELLING IT

All I remember is it was a boring speech—except for one statement. The speaker said it a second time, only louder, probably for the benefit of me and others who had dozed off.

"The better you can say it or write it, the further you can go."

I don't remember who he was, or the occasion. It was not a class. It might have been an after-dinner speech, but those words have proved to be true for me and many friends. They refer to speaking or writing "it." In that statement, "it" is whatever *message* I want to express so that my listeners or readers understand. *Speaking and writing* are how we transmit our thoughts, ideas, and feelings to friends, students, employees, members of organizations, and other responsible people. We use speeches, personal conversation, texting, emails, phone calls, letters, signs, books, journals, and articles to capture readers' and listeners' attention so we can send messages to them.

This is where I had a problem. I think others have a similar problem when it comes to speaking or writing. The problem can cause us to have doubts about ourselves, discouragement, and loss of self-confidence. I know! I have plenty of personal experience to back me up! The lack of self-confidence we can suffer from this problem can cause us to give up a lofty goal or to lower hopes and expectations we had for ourselves.

The fundamental problem is: *It's hard to compose our thoughts*.

Circumstances evolve where we want to transmit a message. It may be good news, a warning, instructions, general information, an opportunity, a threat, or bad news. When that was me, it didn't matter what the subject was—I got excited! How should I begin? How should I say it or write it? I found myself in the proverbial sea without an oar!

My problem would be exposed like this: I could be exploding with excitement because I had good news to tell! It should ignite my listeners and readers, and also make *them* explode with excitement! But they often reacted like store-window dummies! I told them everything that had set me on fire—but they didn't burn! I had not composed a message that transferred my excitement to them. I might as well have read them last week's weather report.

There were days on my job that I had to write an article or discuss a topic that I knew *nothing* about. Rather than copy what someone else wrote about the subject and give them full credit (it's called research) or steal it and write it like it was my own without giving credit to the source (It's called plagiarism), I felt obligated to contribute an original discussion—but how? It was blank page experience, and panic followed. That was resolved later when I found out *how to compose my thoughts and create a message*—even applied to something I didn't know anything about.

How I Learned to Compose a Message

I learned how to compose a message from an unlikely experience. The source was someone I doubted could tell me anything useful. But my first impression was wrong. I attended a breakout session at a writer's conference. The leader was a young nurse who told how her first book was marketed by a major publisher the first time her agent submitted it! (Usually manuscripts are rejected multiple times before a publisher accepts them.) As she told her story, I knew this was exactly what I needed to hear.

She appeared ordinary for a published author! Her manner was humble and soft-spoken as she described her passion to write a book telling *how to become a nurse* for people considering the profession.

However, she was discouraged before she ever began writing, because there were too many topics with too many details that she wanted to include racing around in her mind. She could not sort them out and compose a descriptive message that would be orderly.

Then someone gave her suggestions on how to capture, organize, and compose her various messages. She used the suggestions to organize and write the book and now she was going to describe the process for us who attended her workshop. I have adopted the process she described and can testify that *composing a message* is no longer a problem for me. I will describe the process for you next, much like she did for us who attended her session.

Process for Composing a Message

The nurse-author describing the process stood before a whiteboard. She took a black marker and drew a circle.

"This is the central idea, topic, theme of what we are writing about. For the overall structure of my book, I wrote 'How to Become a Nurse' in the middle of the circle."

CENTRAL IDEA   (HOW TO BECOME A NURSE)

Then she said,

"Anyone can draw a circle (almost) and write a topic inside it, depending on what you want to talk or write about. Or for an exercise, you can pick *any* topic. Pick up a magazine or newspaper—look for a key word, like *camping*, or *cooking*, or *sailing*, or *anything*. You don't have to know *anything* about it, but you can compose a message about it if you follow this method."

Then she went on to say, "The next thing I did was to begin attaching other circles. Each circle stood for a question people might ask about nursing. As quick as the questions popped into my head I put them in a circle or drew a new one. These were questions that needed to be addressed, like 'Who can be a nurse?' 'What does nursing involve?' 'Why should someone become a nurse?' "

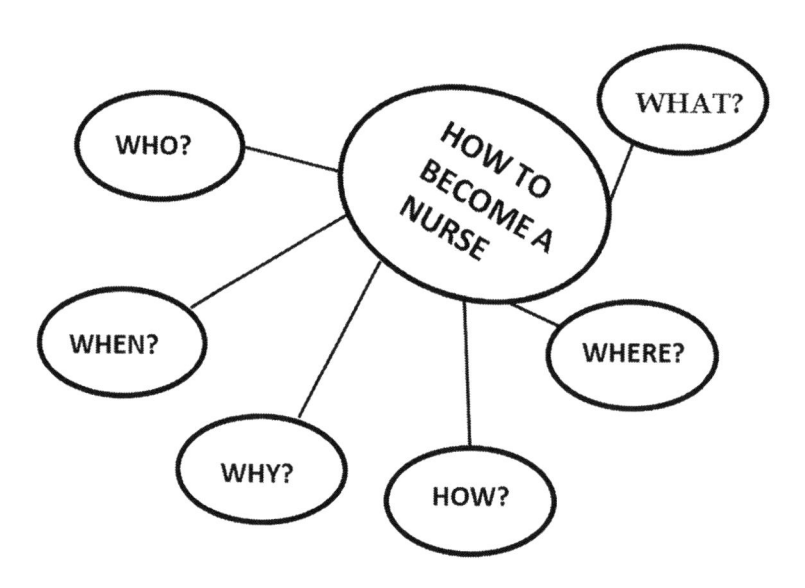

1. Who can be a nurse?
2. What does nursing involve?
3. Why should someone become a nurse?
4. How does someone become a nurse?
5.
6.

"Every circle would likely have several discussion points, each of which occupies separate circles, for example…"

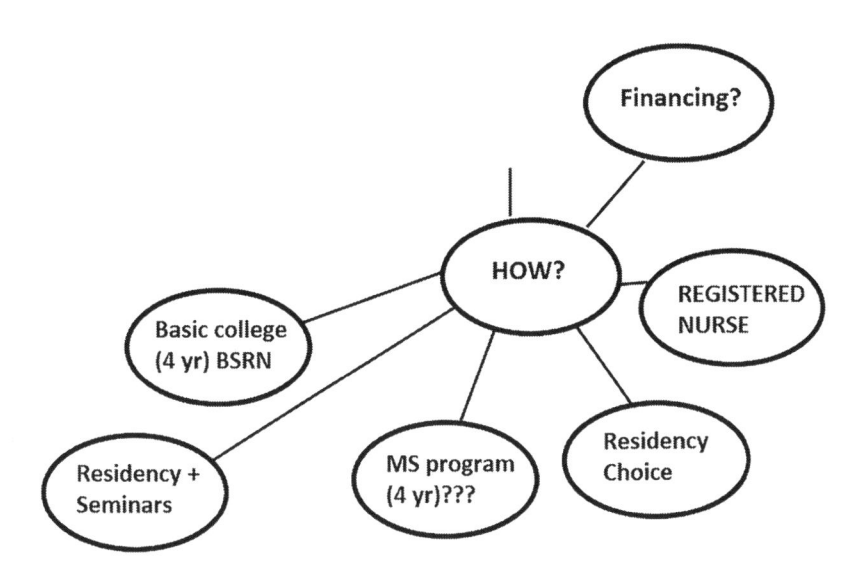

```
                    Financing?
                        |
              HOW? ——— REGISTERED
             / | | \         NURSE
Basic college / | | \
(4 yr) BSRN  /  | |  Residency
            /   | |   Choice
Residency + MS program
Seminars    (4 yr)???
```

She was effectively drawing a *map* of what was in her mind on what was involved in becoming a nurse. Some call a process like this "*mind mapping*," but everyone develops their own version of it. The objective is to get ideas on paper as they pop into your mind and link them with related ideas then or later, but capturing them in a circle before they get away. Some ideas only flash on and off for a moment, and this method helps trap them before they disappear. Our minds work faster than we can write. The nurse-author kept drawing circles with topics that had to be included as she thought of them, and she connected the circles with other circles already on the map at that time or later.

"Ideas from the far corners of your diagram can be moved to where they belong but you may want to wait until the map is saturated or until it seems complete, or until your mind runs dry. Now you have all the pieces to compose your message."

Putting the Message Together

"What are you supposed to do with page(s) covered with interconnected circles, each containing words describing a topic or subtopic to be discussed?"

She waited for an answer, but gave one of her own.

"Look for the best starting point! Identify what will capture attention of the audience. What will help them focus on their need for what you want to tell them. Select what will make them want to hear more because it is important to them. Write sentences and paragraphs from the associated circles, taking time to pick a reasonable order of the information contained. Cross off each circle as it is used, then go on to another circle. When all connected circles contributing to the starting point are crossed out, you have completed the starting point and are ready to go on to the next point."

I use the method just described in composing most of my speeches or chapters. The figure on the last page of this chapter shows my map for a chapter called *The Perfect Crime?* It's about a *dark* incident in my high school years that happened so long ago that I don't mind telling about it now. My recall of it is sharp, and each part of it *rose to the surface* so fast that the only way to capture it was to write key words in separate circles on the page.

I started it with the solid black circle that says, *Innocent as Charged but Guilty in Fact*. The first cluster of circles numbered from (1) to (4) introduce my unfriendly neighbor and her threatening my dog. Circles (5) to (7) give my reaction to her threat. Circles (8) to (11) explain why I had a can of red paint. Circles (12) to (17) describe my friend and I walking to a movie, wearing coats and gloves (it was cold). I threw the red paint on her white house for revenge.

I did not draw the circles in this exact order, but rather as the key thoughts popped into my mind and I had to get them out on the page. The connections and numbered order came later.

Circles (18) to (25) tell about the police detective coming to our house investigating a complaint. He wanted to see my hands. I showed them to him and he was satisfied that there was no red paint on them. I was pronounced *innocent*. However, circles (26) to (32) described how

I began to feel bad about that action some years later. My conscience came alive and would not give me peace until I admitted to myself that what I did was wrong. Then personal peace came. Today, conscience guides my decisions. Thank God for conscience.

The chapter, *The Perfect Crime?*, written in conjunction with the *map* immediately follows after the map itself.

Let all things be done decently and in order.
(I Corinthians 14:40)

> This chapter was included to illustrate a method of composing one's thoughts for a letter, essay, conversation, article, chapter, speech, or book. You may already have a method for written and spoken communication and do not need tips or helps like the ones offered here. Consider yourself fortunate. Otherwise, you may find the method of "Mind Mapping" valuable.

Frederick J. Moody

EXAMPLE "MIND-MAP"

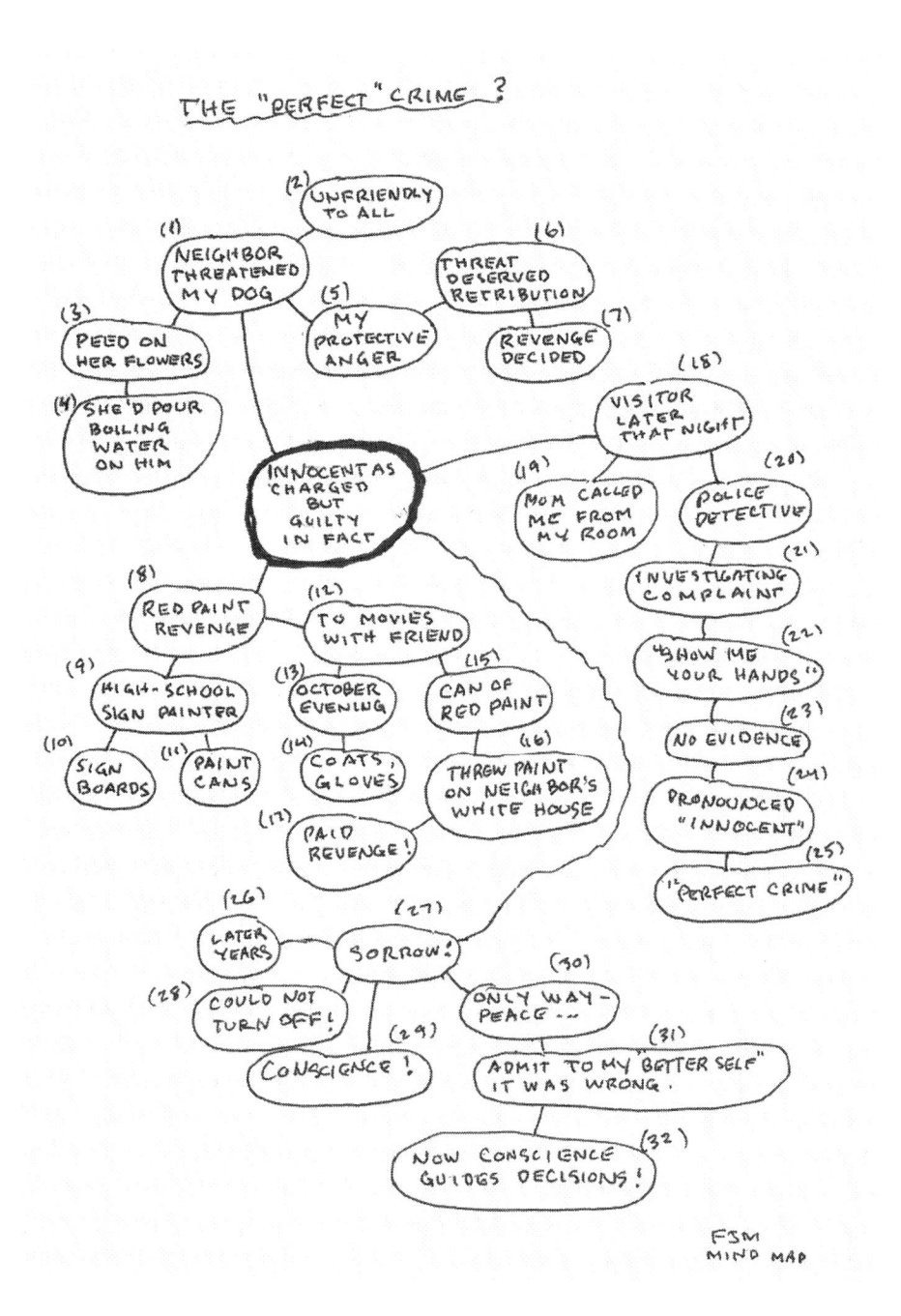

THE "PERFECT" CRIME?

(1) NEIGHBOR THREATENED MY DOG
(2) UNFRIENDLY TO ALL
(3) PEED ON HER FLOWERS
(4) SHE'D POUR BOILING WATER ON HIM
(5) MY PROTECTIVE ANGER
(6) THREAT DESERVED RETRIBUTION
(7) REVENGE DECIDED

INNOCENT AS CHARGED BUT GUILTY IN FACT

(18) VISITOR LATER THAT NIGHT
(19) MOM CALLED ME FROM MY ROOM
(20) POLICE DETECTIVE
(21) INVESTIGATING COMPLAINT
(22) "SHOW ME YOUR HANDS"
(23) NO EVIDENCE
(24) PRONOUNCED "INNOCENT"
(25) "PERFECT CRIME"

(8) RED PAINT REVENGE
(9) HIGH-SCHOOL SIGN PAINTER
(10) SIGN BOARDS
(11) PAINT CANS
(12) TO MOVIES WITH FRIEND
(13) OCTOBER EVENING
(14) COATS, GLOVES
(15) CAN OF RED PAINT
(16) THREW PAINT ON NEIGHBOR'S WHITE HOUSE
(17) PAID REVENGE!

(26) LATER YEARS
(27) SORROW!
(28) COULD NOT TURN OFF!
(29) CONSCIENCE!
(30) ONLY WAY — PEACE...
(31) ADMIT TO MY "BETTER SELF" IT WAS WRONG.
(32) NOW CONSCIENCE GUIDES DECISIONS!

FJM MIND MAP

CHAPTER 40

THE "PERFECT CRIME?"

"If your dog pees on my flowers one more time, I'll pour boiling water on him!" Mrs. Hubbard would do it, too. She was a neighbor two houses down from me that went out of her way to make enemies with every neighbor on our street! She found fault with all of us. Snow blowers and lawnmowers made too much noise. Smoke purposely blew toward her house from burning leaves in the fall. Outdoor recordings of *Rudolph the Red Nosed Reindeer* by Gene Autry at Christmas disturbed her. Little kids banging on their toy drums while they played *holiday parades* upset her. And now my dog! She threatened my dog!

Mrs. Hubbard may have been justified for being upset, but her vile threat called for retaliation! I could have offered to send my dog over to fertilize her precious flowers for fifty cents, but I did not want to offer anything nice. She deserved something to even the score for such a threat. It didn't take long for me to dream up appropriate revenge.

I was in my second year of high school and was earning extra money by painting signs for small businesses. My room was filled with plywood boards of all sizes, paintbrushes, and dozens of cans filled with colored paint. A friend and I decided to walk downtown to see a movie that Friday evening. It was late October and cold enough to wear coats and gloves. I also took a partly full can of red enamel. As we passed Mrs. Hubbard's white house, with no light but the streetlight, I threw red paint on the side of Mrs. Hubbard's white porch. "That should balance the scales," I thought to myself as we continued on to the movie, and I tossed the empty can into a pile of raked leaves.

When I came home later that evening, I was in my room working on some art project and our doorbell rang. I could hear my mother talking with a man downstairs. She called and asked me to come down. I met a man in the living room, standing tall in a topcoat with a badge. He introduced himself as a police detective who had been called out to investigate a complaint in our neighborhood. I was too preoccupied with my upstairs project to even connect the red paint incident with his mission. He said, "May I see your hands?" Without hesitation I held both hands out to him where he examined them closely, looking at each finger—both sides, the palms, front and back, and finally put them down at my sides. "It's fine. We get so many calls from that woman every week, complaining about various neighbors. Sorry I bothered you. She didn't directly accuse you, but someone put red paint on her white house." He said "Good night," and left. That was that. (It occurred to me much later that I was glad he did not want to examine the gloves I had been wearing earlier!)

My mother told me later that when the detective had told her why he had come, she was worried that I might have been involved because I had so many cans of colored paint. Then she said, "When I saw how fast you showed him your hands, I had no more doubts that you couldn't be the one!" I never upset her with further voluntary information. She died never knowing, and so did everyone else!

That is, everyone else except me and my friend, and he never tattled! Some years later, it was like a dormant part of me inside woke up and made me feel bad about what I did. I could not shake it! I knew it was wrong, and it began to bother me. I wondered how to get rid of the feeling, but it wouldn't go away! Then it dawned—I had discovered my *conscience*! Never before had it been this active! But now I had to find some way to fix the continuous distress that it made. It was simple. My conscience would quit pressuring me if I did one thing: If I admitted to myself that what I did was wrong! I wasn't Catholic so I didn't go to confession, but I made a sort of *self-confession and told God I was sorry*. A realization that there are actions my *better self* does not want to permit. *Conscience* is there to prevent those actions. Thank you God for *conscience*.

Your ears shall hear a word behind you, saying, "This is the way, walk in it," whenever you turn to the right hand or whenever you turn to the left. (*Isaiah 30:21*)

>On what occasion did you discover you had a conscience? The Bible notes that those who live by lies can destroy their conscience. (*"..speaking lies in hypocrisy, having their own conscience seared with a hot iron,"* I Timothy 4:2). When I have lied, usually on the spur of the moment, I feel an instant sense of conviction. Thank God for that. I won't even ask if your experience is similar.

CHAPTER 41

PERSPECTIVE

I once had a dream about two backpackers caught in a violent mountain storm, running to find shelter. When the storm passed, they emerged from a thicket into the densely populated forest. They had lost their compass, cellphones, and maps. The sky was still dark with clouds so that they could not locate the sun. They were lost. With no hint of clear skies, there was no hope of stars to guide them when night came either. Every direction looked the same—trees and underbrush.

One of the hikers climbed a tree. Nearing the top, he called out, "I see a trail!" His *perspective* changed from a ground view to an elevated view. Both hikers followed the trail, and walked out of the forest. *Perspective* changed their condition from *ignorance*—lost, not knowing the way out, to *understanding*—found, knowing how to leave the forest.

I had a problem

I was looking forward to the weekend one sunny Friday afternoon as I parked on the Stanford campus. Three times a week I commuted for a math class. The class was interesting, but so were the anecdotes of Professor Wilhelm Flugge, who had defected with his wife, Irmgard Flugge Lotz, from Hitler's Germany. Both were Stanford professors who had been forced to design airfoils for the German Luftwaffe (air weapon). They secretly traveled to America to find freedom in the U. S. I was privileged to have both of them as instructors.

I have tried to forget the pain of the brutal homework assignments he dumped on us. The following is an approximate example: Professor

Flugge began with a German accent, "Eet's yur job to kekulate dee streess profeel in da theek, kurve weendow mit dee *'feenite eelement meethod'* uf Strang, Feex, und Zienkiewicz." He handed each of us the homework problem for this week. I groaned. The curved window he wanted us to analyze was probably for a deep-dive submarine carrying two scientists five to seven miles down to study the ocean floor in the Mariana Trench. If the window crushed under high external pressure, both men on board would die instantly. Being squashed to death didn't upset me as much as anticipating the monotonous hours it would take for the homework, which we had to do by hand.

The numerical method would be slow-going, checking and double-checking, dull and boring—especially because I was surrounded at work by energetic engineering assistants who were ready to help me at the slightest call. But I had to do the labor and endure the agony myself to pass the class. So I ground on, waking up in an upset state of mind every morning with the absurd assignment mocking me.

I knew I had a problem. To be upset for a short time from a lousy homework assignment or when something came along that I did not like, would be normal. But to remain upset day and night was unnatural. This was not the first time I suffered like this. Whenever something came along that I did not like, it made me unhappy, and sometimes depressed, angry, upset, unmotivated, often for long periods.

Yes, there are things we should dislike, e.g., an ingrown toenail. There are bad influences which entice people to cheat, bully others, abuse weaker ones, rob victims, lie, and cause damage. I remember one overgrown brat of a third-grader at a summer daycamp where I was a counselor one year. He said, "Mithter Moody, did you get the letter I thent you?" I thought he was serious and asked, "What letter?" He said, "I geth I forgot to put a thtamp on it!" and he slammed his heavy foot down on mine. I yelled because it hurt, but I was able to hold back the bad words, and he ran beyond my reach, which likely saved his life that day! Anyway, most things that upset me were not necessarily evil or bad, but rather those things I did not like and wanted to avoid—like Flugge's homework.

I tried to avoid anything I did not like. I became an expert *avoider*. If a group was picking volunteers for something I didn't like, I found a reason to be absent while they picked a volunteer. If they thought I was the best person for something I didn't like, I already had composed a conflict that would disqualify me. "I already have a commitment at that time," (which probably was working on one of my own projects) or "I'll be out of town—sorry!" If I couldn't avoid being *drafted* into *something* I didn't like, I warned the *drafters* that I was over-committed and couldn't devote the effort the particular *something* deserved. If they ignored my excuse and dumped the job on me anyway, I ignored the job or purposely messed it up. When someone complained, I reminded them that I had said I couldn't handle it with my other commitments. They found someone "to help Fred" or "to take the load off him." I usually did not get *a second chance* to mess up a job dumped on me that I didn't like.

The Flugge homework assignment involved monotonous calculations. I could only boil in anger while I plowed through the numbers! Daily anger was eating me up inside.

I had to do something about my problem, which I could describe as follows:

(1) Something happened (the cause)
(2) That made me unhappy (the effect)
(3) My unhappiness could lead to personal damage (the result)

When I am *unhappy*, it can make me *bitter*, and *bitterness can do damage*. Consider the life principle in the Bible that says,

Pursue peace with all people, and holiness, without which no one will see the Lord; looking carefully lest anyone fall short of the grace

of God; lest any ROOT OF BITTERNESS springing up cause trouble, and by this many become defiled.
(Hebrews 12:14,15—capitalization mine)

Unhappiness is linked to *anger, fear, grief, and/or depression*, all of which involve a level of *bitterness*, or *hostility*. I can feel *bitterness* releasing something like acid internally that resembles burning which is *damaging my physical and emotional health. My spiritual peace and well-being* are getting bruised and burned at the same time. Therefore, the unhappiness state should be fixed as soon as possible.

I want to fix my problem to prevent consequences to myself or others. The *thing* that caused damage may have happened minutes ago, hours, days, or months ago, but damage has a way of progressing unless it is stopped. My optimism insists that this problem can be fixed by answering, "What Should I Do Now?"

Fixing the problem

I already described my problem with these three parts:

(1) Something happened (the cause)
(2) That made me unhappy (the effect)
(3) My unhappiness could lead to personal damage (the result)

That's the *cause—effect--result* description. Something happened (*the cause*); That made me unhappy (*the effect*); My unhappiness could lead to personal damage (*the result*) by making me bitter, and bitterness can do physical, emotional, and spiritual damage, not always limited to myself. I can hurt others by things I say and do if I let my unhappiness run loose.

Before trying to fix any problem, it is good to examine each part of the problem. Consider the first few words of the problem:

Something happened..: I don't have control over all the things that happen. A storm, an earthquake, a red traffic light, a flat tire, a death in the family, lost keys or wallet, or I get passed over for a raise or promotion, someone else gets the credit for something I did, I get sick, or a hundred other possible things that I didn't expect or plan for. *I cannot change some things that happen.* (I may try to change their effect, but that doesn't change the fact that they happen.)

The next few words are:

...that made me unhappy (the effect): **T**here were times when I learned more about *something* that changed my *perspective*. Things looked different to me as I learned more about them. (In some sense, I climbed a tree and discovered a path!) I began to *like something I didn't like!* Because my reaction became so different, I might have to admit I was wrong at first. That could hurt my pride because I thought it would make me look weak and less brilliant than I wanted people to think I was, and that's humiliating. But the alternative was to be dishonest with others and myself, which was worse!

Then the light shined!

Whenever I heard someone admit they were wrong, they didn't look weak to me. Instead, I thought they looked strong, courageous, honest, and their integrity score went high on my score sheet! They were not afraid to let others know that they did not think of themselves more highly than they ought to think, but rather that they were as vulnerable to imperfections as anyone, and were not always 100 percent right! They were like us! When a speaker or writer identifies with us who are their audience, we are more likely to hear their message, which usually contains profound information we need to hear.

From that point, I have wanted to learn all I could about anything I didn't like in order to get a more complete perspective. Whenever a better perspective causes me to like what I previously disliked, the value of a better perspective proves itself.

Therefore, one way to fix the problem is...

"to increase our perspective of the thing we don't like.."

Part (2) of the problem no longer exists when our "dislike" has changed to "like."

An example where perspective changed me from "don't like" to "like" happened one afternoon:

"What Did I Do?"

I was designated as a mentor for young engineers who were in their first five years with the company. This meant spending time with them, discussing their problems, and helping them find job assignments that would contribute to their long-term goals. Discussing their futures with them took many hours. I had my own projects that needed attention, and time spent with the young engineers often put me behind, making it necessary to work on weekends. The "honor" of being a mentor was more like a "curse" at times.

Having spent most of the morning with two mentees, I thought I could spend the afternoon on a report that was needed by next week. That explains why I didn't like it when George rushed into my cubicle, extremely distressed. "What did I do?" He handed me a layoff notice! GE CEO Jack Welch had sent out instructions that managers should get rid of 10 percent of their staff"...to get rid of *dead wood*, as he put it. This was his way of *managing by fear* that theoretically kept employees functioning at better-than-their-best. However, one "freshman" manager didn't know that new engineers like George were exempt from layoffs. He didn't know that George was a recent hire, so he laid him off. The damage was done, and couldn't be reversed.

My first thought was, "This interruption is taking me away from something I need to do—something I planned to do—and now I have to delay it again!" I was upset, thinking I could send George to a section manager to sort out his dilemma. But he was more upset than I was. I realized, "Here is a young man who has been wrongfully fired from his job for no fault of his. I know the phony reason behind it, and I am his first line of defense to help correct it." My *perspective* began to shift off myself and completely onto George and how we were going to undo this unforgiveable action. The paperwork was already processed, so the layoff was irreversible. Now I was in George's corner and putting on the *gloves*.

I spent the next two days getting George re-hired and re-assigned to another group. This was *damage control* to fix the ignorance of a young manager who must have been too proud to ask a senior manager for advice. It was *pick up the pieces* with no particular benefit for me—I lost more time that should have gone to my project, which I ended up finishing at home over the weekend. The benefit was a happy new engineer, who stayed employed and said he liked his new job assignment better than the one he had when he was laid off.

By examining my perspective, my initial "I don't like this" reaction had changed into a challenge that *I did like* because of the fulfilling result..

Bear one another's burdens, and so fulfill the law of Christ. (Galatians 6:2)

George must have told his dad, who was a professor of international fame. Without my knowledge, (and maybe just to show appreciation) this well-known "professor-above-scale" at his university successfully nominated me for induction into the *National Academy of Engineering* (NAE), an engineering organization of renown. I had seen no personal benefit in helping George. Becoming a member of the NAE has opened doors of opportunity for teaching, consulting, and technical seminars, which have provided forums for the *deeper things of life*. NAE membership has included well-known engineers, like *(pardon the name-dropping, but I do it to prove a point)* Steve Jobs (Apple), Jack Welch (GE), Lee Iacocca (General Motors), Bill Gates (Microsoft),

WHAT SHOULD I DO NOW?

Steve Wozniak (Chief Scientist, Primary Data), Erik Schmidt (former VP Google), Ed Hood (GE), Nancy Fitzroy (GE), and hundreds of famous engineers, researchers, professors, and scientific founders who are known for significant roles in moving technology forward, (and me, who took pity on the son of an influential NAE member). The point is that I think it proves God has a sense of humor! "Fred who?"

> Have you received recognition or an award at some time? Was it in competition, based on service, or achievement, or other criteria? What were some group comments? How did you actually feel about the event? How would you answer if someone asked you to answer truthfully about how you felt?

APPENDIX

This is a summary-outline of the optional talk I have given to my graduate and undergraduate classes at San Jose State University, and also for invited keynote speeches at engineering banquets and celebrations.

I cannot claim originality for these "laws" because there is no single source where they are listed that I can name. Rather, they came from speeches given by CEOs at company-wide meetings, or from offhand comments I found in books intended to inspire readers to reach maximum performance, or from collected Proverbs of Solomon, still upheld for his wisdom.

SEVEN LAWS OF SUCCESS
(Speaking of the people who follow these laws)

They are like a tree planted by streams of water,
Which yields its fruit in season
And whose leaf does not wither.
Whatever they do prospers. (Psalms 1:3)

1. **LEARN TO GET EXCITED ABOUT YOUR WORK (A good attitude can turn most assignments into life-building experiences.)**

Some work assignments may be enjoyable, but it is most likely that some assignments will be dull, boring, and of no real significance. If you treat each assignment as if it is of the highest importance, imagining that the success or failure of the particular project depends on you doing an excellent job on it, you will find yourself becoming excited about what you are doing. Your attitude will be noticed and when it is consistent, it will result in remarkable career feedback.

2. **USE OR LOSE (Generous use of personal abilities insures continued growth.)**

   Continue to remind yourself of your personal talents and abilities, thinking of ways you might use them in your present work assignment or in the idea you are trying to promote.

3. **PRODUCE TO PERFECTION (Carrying each assignment to completion brings career satisfaction.)**

   Sometimes there is a temptation to "almost" finish a job if there are insignificant "loose ends" or details dangling out there. No one will notice if those items are finished or not and they would take significant effort to complete. If you pay attention to these details, you will have done an "extraordinary job" rather than an "ordinary job." You will find greater satisfaction in becoming known as one who does extraordinary work.

4. **GIVE TO GET (Giving, not getting, increases personal capacity to produce.)**

   Some think what they give, they lose. What they don't realize is that the right kind of giving becomes an investment. Most people with a gift, ability, or talent are eager to exercise it in a way that benefits others. You will likely find opportunities in a job assignment to apply something you can do that was not required in the job description. You may be able to read or speak a foreign language, which makes it possible to bring in a participant from another country or foreign published work to help obtain a solution to a current problem, or you may have artistic skills to help compose a presentation. The list goes on.

5. **WELCOME NEW EXPERIENCES (New experiences prevent career stagnation.)**

   Some work assignments may cause anxiety because they are out of your experience and you fear you might fail. It means stepping out of your *comfort zone* into new territory with no safety net. You can choose to be miserable throughout the new assignment, or you can decide to be glad for it, knowing that the stress from functioning in the new territory builds personal strength so you can handle new challenges and never stagnate in your career.

6. **HAVE FLEXIBLE PLANS (Expecting that even the best plans may change helps prevent frustration.)**

Most plans are composed of separate pieces, each of which has a probability of failure. Some key element may not arrive or happen in time. Some key player may get sick. Some device may burn out or stop working. Any of the separate failures may doom the total plan—unless you have an alternate—a Plan B! The problem is that some plans seem fail-proof and a Plan B seems unnecessary. Sad experiences have shown that you should always be ready to pivot and follow a different plan because you know that because you live in an imperfect world you will encounter an ambush now and then where you need to be flexible and change plans.

7. **THINK "MOTIVATION" (Worthwhile motivation leads to a lifetime fulfillment.)**

You may be motivated by a given assignment because you see it as an opportunity to learn something of interest to you. When that is the case, you will readily give enthusiastic effort to the job at hand. What about an assignment that is the least interesting, and you see it is of no value to you or your career? That is when your imagination can come to your rescue: you can IMAGINE what you might gain from the assignment that could have a positive effect on your makeup. Enjoy the exposure! Whenever you gain knowledge outside of your primary interests, you are growing, and that can be highly motivating.

EPILOGUE
(Included by permission from Chuck H.)

My friend Chuck H. said he heard his dad and grandfather downstairs Christmas Eve after he had gone to bed. They were swearing, not at each other, but at something else. Chuck got up and quietly started down the steps, but he stopped. The two men were assembling a bicycle. Across the handlebars was a sign: "Merry Christmas from Santa."

He stared at that sign and the two men working with wrenches and screwdrivers. He thought, "They told me there was a Santa Claus, but that was a lie! There is no Santa Claus!" Later, his reasoning extended to God, as his family members were devout Catholics. "They told me there is a God, but that might be a lie, too."

Chuck had been raised in parochial school, and continued to have increasing doubts. One day his father came home raging against the church. "They take your money to get you into heaven, then when you die they take your money to get you out of purgatory! I'm done with the church!" That sealed it for Chuck. Thereafter, he claimed to be an atheist.

Chuck had a Bible-believing grandmother who cared about his eternal destination and regularly explained in specific detail that God loved him and sent Jesus to die for his sins in order to forgive him and give him the gift of eternal life. But Chuck didn't believe any of it. His Grandma told him, in her own loving way, that if he did not believe in Jesus, he would burn forever in hell. Chuck told me that Grandma probably would look over the edge of heaven some day to see him burning in hell and say, "Chucky, I told you so!"

Chuck and I have talked long hours mostly at various Starbucks locations. He knows that I love him and am hoping that he would take Granny's pleading advice, because I also know the peace and assurance that comes through belief in Jesus. Chuck admits to our being "created" but not by the God of the Bible. He attributes our existence to distant aliens who are extremely advanced to the point where they created the human race, and who knows what else? But not a God who holds us accountable for sin and casts anyone into a lake of fire. Try as he might, Chuck says he cannot believe that Someone Who claimed to be the Son of God died for him to save him from his sin, death, and hell; rose from the dead, in order to offer him the free gift of eternal life in heaven with Himself.

Chuck listens when I offer "a reason for the hope that is within me," and he does not argue or condemn my unshakeable belief in a scripture promise like:

For God so loved the world that He gave His only begotten Son, that whosoever believes in Him should not perish but have everlasting life. (John 3:16)

Chuck is a kind, generous human being, who has helped people of low financial resources achieve their dreams, paid the complex surgery bill for people living in the shadows, and helped raise large sums for organizations like Stanford Medical that bring a future hope to the hopeless. I tell him that he does not have to believe exactly like I do, but that if he received Christ into his life, he would see his own lovingkindness multiplied with new life of eternal extent. When I assure him that I continue to pray for him, he says, "It won't hurt."

FJM, 2024

FULL READER REACTIONS

Fred writes again a series of life experiences that entertain us and bring a deeper understanding of who he is and how he has developed his life experiences into teachings, guidance, and thoughts on life itself and how to handle the many obstacles and uncertain events that occur to all of us. He gives his perspective on how he handled some of his own (or close friend's) events and what lessons they learned, what trials they caused and the knowledge to move on and help others needing support in their own struggles and uncertainties. It is so valuable to give others a sense that they are not alone and many share similar issues. Fred's entertaining style helps us view our own life experiences and look into how we asked ourselves: "What Should I Do Now?" and gauge how we did. His writings bring up our own old memories and actions and help us laugh at ourselves for some of our actions. Fred's scripture references uniquely show the value of these life lessons. I thoroughly enjoyed the book. I've known and worked with Fred for over 30 years and have valued not only his unique Engineering problem solving skills, but more importantly his long-lasting friendship and desire to help others satisfy their life's challenges and understand these events and learn how to meet the challenges and become better individuals for this guidance and support.--*Steven A. Hucik, Vice President and General Manager (retired), GE Hitachi Nuclear Energy.*

In small vignettes, Fred recounts his life lessons such as getting the facts, evaluating the consequences, and wisely applying to life experiences and relationships.--R*ev. Lamar Allen, MST & M. Div.*

Dr. Fred Moody graciously and humorously shares several life stories with us, infused with Biblical wisdom. You will find the right one for your current season of life. --D*awn Standart, HR Director for large social service non-profit; wife, mother, Christian, life-long learner.*

Fred Moody's "What Should I Do Now?" is a masterpiece that captures the essence of life's pivotal moments through the lens of a seasoned storyteller and master communicator. As my mentor in Toastmasters, Fred has always provided invaluable advice and the book is no exception. His ability to weave humor and wisdom into every page makes the book not only an enlightening read but also an enjoyable one. A man of faith but not a preacher, Fred's insights resonate deeply, offering ideas and motivational thoughts simply through his words. His unique talent for making others feel good about themselves shines through in his writing, leaving readers both inspired and entertained. Whether you're seeking guidance or just a good laugh, "What Should I Do Now?" is a must read.—*Pete O'Bryan, Sergeant, U. S. Air Force, 1966-1970; Manager, Foster Farms as Manager, 43 yrs., Nat. Council of Weights & Measures; currently Distinguished Toastmaster—three terms as Area Director.*

I have read the draft copy of "What Should I Do Now?" and found that it was interesting and well-written. I know the author even better now and I wish him well in the days ahead. I am not sure who his intended audience is, but I guess it is the Evangelical Christian Community. I doubt that it will be a NY Times best seller. (Dr. Lahey enclosed helpful editorial comments.) Good luck with the book, Fred. I hope my minor edits are helpful to you. Be good and stay well.--*Good friend and a former GE colleague, Dick Lahey, Edward E. Hood Emeritus Professor of Engineering at Rensselaer Polytechnic Institute (RPI); currently Trustee of the Unitarian Universalist Fellowship of St. Augustine, Florida.*

It was one of these books that captures your interest with a "SO WHAT" in affecting me. What decisions do I need to make? How is God in His love rooting for and guiding me? As Fred shared many good and difficult life experiences, I wonder how I would have responded? How is God in His love rooting for and guiding me?? Retreating or charging ahead trusting God through each circumstance? Each chapter has relevant Bible verses connecting with me as a challenge or a promise. This is a book that will challenge us to daily apply God's Word to our lives. --*Bruce Burman, Retired VP of Semiconductor Corp.*

I enjoyed your latest and most inspiring work. I started reading it and could not put it down until I finished it! God has given you a wonderful gift of communicating and sharing encouraging words with others. I love your interaction of including humor with making clear and understandable points. --D*ale Isaac, Director, Audit Division California Franchise Tax Board, Retired* .

It is my privilege to endorse the book, "What Should I Do Now?" written by Dr. Frederick J. Moody. Whenever we face some challenge in life, this is the first question we must answer. Dr. Moody has vividly described his life experiences in this book. Each chapter of the book describes some life challenge and successfully demonstrates the author's approach to answer the question using not only his physical knowledge and understanding of the challenge but also the spiritual wisdom gained through application of Biblical principles. While most people apply their personal knowledge and understanding of the situation to answer the question, "What Should I Do Now?" when they face challenges in life, it is the integration of one's approach with the wisdom gained through Biblical principles, that determines the successful outcome of our efforts to meet our challenges. The book is a major contribution to encourage and motivate the present and the future generations to confidently deal with the challenges of life. --*Dr. Shyam Dua, Manager, GENE Engineering Quality (Retired) & Director, San Jose BWR Engineering Operations, Westinghouse (Retired)*

Having read the previous two books by this author, once again Dr. Moody has shared some precious examples and Biblical responses to many of the same trials that we all face as human beings in a fallen world. Such trials can often be a "blessing in disguise" which are only realized later. His near-photographic memory of life experiences is amazing and his sense of humor is refreshing. As a fellow believer and engineer, his ability to communicate with wisdom and compassion for the people encountered is impressive. The examples and solutions described are very practical and not just theoretical. I was reminded of something learned long ago as a fellow technologist: It helps to get through trials in our career by remembering that we work for the Lord at our employers and hence trust in His care and guidance. Of course it always helps to prepare with knowledge and education, but understanding and wisdom come with experience and acknowledgement of God's leading and intervention in our lives. The blessing of Godly wives and long marriages is something else that Dr. Moody and I have in common. Our wives were an example of those described in Proverbs 31, and they contributed greatly with their love and support to our families. While we carry on without them, a wise person once advised, "We know where they are." May this book help each reader benefit from the knowledge, understanding, and wisdom contained within its pages. --*Dr. David F. Kyser, Ph.D. Electrical Engineering, San Jose, CA.*

Dr. Moody's book is full of his real-life experiences that we can all identify with, in some way or another, as if they're our stories as well. What makes how he shares his life so different from others is his willingness to look deeply into the events of his life with rigorous honesty, vulnerability and humility. Fred knows where he's been and sees how his life experiences have shaped him into the man that he is today, and that reflects the character of God. Each of his life stories is rife with insights, wisdom, and infused with principles from God's Word. He writes with some humor and a touch of sarcasm, and that makes him real. After reading his book you will feel like you've just experienced an elegant dinner! --*Dr. Robert A. Johns, O.D., F.A.A.O.*

What Should I Do Now is a captivating read that feels like a casual conversation with a friend over coffee or donuts. Fred's storytelling prowess, validated by his eighth-grade English teacher, shines through every page as he shares his personal journey. Each anecdote is infused with raw emotion, covering topics from family to work relationships, all while incorporating sound Biblical principles without being preachy. With Fred's relatable storytelling, the book offers not only entertainment but also valuable insights for navigating life's challenges. –*Sam Paulissian, Distinguished Toastmaster*

This is a work teeming with rich life principles, sprinkled with humor as when Dr. Moody was a poor university student and he bought his wife to be, Phyllis, an engagement ring in which he said the diamond was so small, it came with a complimentary magnifying glass. He unashamedly opens his life, pulling back the curtain and he draws us in like a magnet with captivating stories and renders us almost incapable of putting the book down. He brings us heart-warming snapshots of difficult circumstances most all of us face, like rejection, disappointment, unfair treatment by a boss, being misunderstood, being scammed, being put down in a meeting and failure on a test. As a skillful story teller, he totally draws us in and we want to be on his team. He wants us to know that no matter what we face, there is always hope. I have witnessed these truths in his life, first hand as a former engineering student in Dr. Moody's fluid mechanics class at San Jose State University, as well as a fellow employee/mentee t GE, and affirm that what he shares is the real Dr. Fred Moody. As I understand it, his ultimate purpose is to demonstrate with honesty and transparency that in the Christian life, the successes as well as the failures are under the tutelage of our loving God. For your life journey as you encounter circumstances, you will find hope as you observe how the author navigates through the obstacles in his life with humor and resolve.—*David S. Licata, BS, MA, MDIV, Life Teaching Credential: Math, Electrical Engineering, Nuclear Power & Aerospace Industries (Ret.) Pres. Emer. The Silicon Valley Engineering Council; Navigators; US Army; husband, father.*

Fred Moody is a delightful story teller, and "What Should I Do Now?" does not disappoint. The book is chuck full of sometimes hilarious, sometimes poignant (often both!) recollections of life experiences. From these very relatable stories, he shares timeless Biblical wisdom that will help anyone encountering similar situations and perplexities that beg the question, "What Should I Do Now?"—*Burford Furman, PhD. Professor, Mechanical Engineering, San Jose State University.*

Mr. Moody's stories of life's daily challenges helped me to realize that we all have situations that can either make or break us. He is a natural storyteller but he didn't always have a positive outcome. As he said, it's not the power of positive thinking, but thinking positively. Each of the stories has a life lesson we can all relate to. The Bible verses enhance these messages. You can read each chapter individually, no need to start from the beginning to end. A real handy book to put a smile on your face or make it easier for you to face daily challenges.—*Sylvia Kisling, Distinguished Toastmaster, (DTM)*

Fred Moody's latest book, "What Should I Do Now?" is not only fun to read but also is enlightening! Each of the chapters, being accounts of Fred's interactions with a wide variety of people, gives insights stemming from interactions with them. In every case Fred learned,(i.e. discovered) something (i.e., knowledge) that led to a better understanding of working with both people and problems. For example, in each case Fred was confronted by the problem of answering the question:"What Should I Do Now?" The end result was always enhanced wisdom. I highly recommend his book. You'll both enjoy reading it and also; I'm quite sure that you will learn more than you ever imagined! --*Richard R. Schultz, Consultant, formerly Idaho National Engineering Laboratory (INEL).*

"What Should I Do Now?" is a powerful book that has helped me to think about life as an endeavor of learning motivating others, and making the best from life's valuable experiences. This book should be mandatory for U. S. College English Critical Thinking Courses. –*Chris D. Hempleman, California Teaching Credential Candidate, Dept. of Social Sciences USC, Rossier School of Education. Valley Home Joint School District Board of Trustees.*

If any of you lack wisdom, let him ask of God, who gives to all liberally and without reproach and it will be given to him. But let him ask in faith, with no doubting, for he who doubts is like a wave of the sea driven and tossed in the wind. (James 1:5,6)

Made in the USA
Middletown, DE
22 October 2024